# Will They Love Me When I Leave?

# Will They Love Me When I Leave?

### A Weekend Father's Struggle to Stay Close to His Kids

## C. W. Smith

G. P. Putnam's Sons    New York

G. P. Putnam's Sons
*Publishers Since 1838*
200 Madison Avenue
New York, NY 10016

*Designed by Rhea Braunstein*

Library of Congress Cataloging-in-Publication Data

Smith, C. W. (Charles William), date.
Will they love me when I leave?

1. Divorced fathers.   2. Father and child.
I. Title.
HQ756.S546   1987      306.8'742      86-25130
ISBN 0-399-13249-X

PRINTED IN THE UNITED STATES OF AMERICA
1   2   3   4   5   6   7   8   9   10

*For my children,*
*to my children,*
*so at least they'll know*
*who their father truly is*

# CONTENTS

# Will They Love Me
# When I Leave?

# INTRODUCTION

This book grew out of an essay that appeared in *Esquire* about my problems as a "divorced" father—I had been a non-custodial parent for five years, and I had been struggling to stay in close touch with my son and daughter. What led me to write it was a need to shape my feelings about the most important trouble in my adult life.

Before that, it hadn't been my habit as a novelist or a journalist to write about myself. And so I wrote this book with my eyes closed, so to speak: I imagined that what I wrote would not be read. To overcome my reticence about making public what my temperament had insisted should remain private, I pretended I was talking only to myself. Such self-delusion would, I thought, lead me to be more honest. It would discourage wishful thinking and squelch the onerous tendency to show only my best face to a reader.

Until the essay was published, my grief and confusion were mine alone, but afterward they seemed, alarmingly, to belong to many. I received dozens of letters from *Esquire* readers expressing pain, bitterness, anger, confusion, and sometimes gratitude for having told my story: that of a father who tries under difficult circumstances to remain important to the children he loves.

Aside from the few nicely penned letters from literate readers writers are grateful to get after publishing a novel, I was unaccustomed to hearing from my audience. The mail I now got felt like an avalanche—not just in quantity and length, but also in the anguish the letters conveyed. Unwittingly, I had become an authority on a particular kind of pain, it seemed, yet in truth I had become an authority only on my own. I answered many of the letters, though usually I felt helpless.

Many letters contained voluminous personal details about legal complications and domestic strife, and their writers were looking for a sympathetic ear. Some asked for advice ("I'm a father of two who's wondering whether to get divorced or not.") and some were angry ("A HUSBAND AND WIFE ARE THE ONLY PEOPLE WHO CAN REACH AN ENDURING AND WHOLESOME AGREEMENT ON HOW THE CHILDREN WILL SPEND THEIR YEARS BECOMING ADULTS!"). A few were angry not at former spouses or the courts, but at me. My essay did not excuse absent or negligent fathers, but simply hearing the side of the non-custodial father, whom I called "Uncle Dad," enraged some custodial mothers.

Most writers, though, were not angry but sad: "My daughter . . . won't speak to me. She's 24. We haven't communicated in nearly a year. My son and I are OK, but much there, too, has been lost and will never be recovered. And I still sometimes feel like a bankrupt father." Still another letter came from a grown daughter who, though not related to the "bankrupt father," gave another side of the story: "At various times in my adult life I have confronted how much it hurt that we didn't have those important times together when we were teenagers and Dad was far away. And I deal with the feelings, and think I'm done with them, and I go on. But occasionally they resurface and I realize that even accepting the pain and loss and disappointment does not dispel them forever."

Nothing was as disturbing, though, as letters that communicated the pain of children who were still suffering. One woman, whose teenage daughter had made two suicide attempts, explained that the girl's father had left their home when she was fourteen months old, remarried, and had three children by his second wife. His visits to the child he had fathered by the writer came only once or twice a year. Once, however, "when she was ten he came and took her skiing with his other three children and his second wife. She, who never talked (a bad sign), came home and said, 'Those children asked me if I had a father and I didn't want to hurt their feelings and tell them he was my father too, so I just said they're divorced.'" The writer added: "Later I had the three of them come for a visit and it went all right, but she never wanted to do it again. She envied them too much."

From all the mail I learned the obvious—that broken families mean broken hearts. I also learned that hearing about someone else's problems is medicinal, and from that I learned that it's not arrogant for me to presume that other people want to hear about my life, or, more accurately, about another person's life, so long as the account of it grapples with the difficult business of being human.

Some people wanted to know more about problems I only hinted at in the essay, and many people felt that it invited questions such as "Why did you have children in the first place?" and "Why did you get divorced?" If such questions were not answered or even raised, it was partly because of the limited scope of the essay—by design, it focused exclusively on the relationship I had as an "Uncle Dad" to my children. In this full-length work, though, I have room to tell perhaps even more than I want. I've widened my original story so that now it concerns making and breaking one small family through divorce, and the difficulty of continuing to be a father after a breakup.

In a way, I'm writing it for the same reasons I wrote the essay—to discover the truth. What I say probably won't repair anything already broken, and it's not calculated to prevent anyone from doing whatever they might have set out to do before reading it. I have no advice to offer. If my story has any merit to justify what some might feel is a self-indulgent exploitation of my own and my family's sadness, it would be that hearing what is true for another person sometimes allows us the balm of consolation. People have a profound longing to belong to nice, solid families like the Cleavers or the Waltons or the Huxtables; this intense yearning explains the popularity of these models, and the popularity lures many into the delusion that they alone belong to stormy, chaotic, torn and miserable families, while all the rest of the world, it seems, sits down peacefully to pot roast on Sunday after joining hands in prayer. The truth is otherwise. The truth is what I've tried to tell.

My former spouse, my present wife and my children have to endure coexistence with this record of their lives written by someone who has never been a truly objective observer, and they cannot adequately explain or defend themselves without access to a similar forum. To protect their privacy as much as possible, I have changed their names, and when what I have to say involves the privacy of others outside my family, I have also taken the liberty of slipping disguises, if you will, over some of the "characters."

# ONE

# Green and Golden

Long before I burned the well-house down, turkeys were raised on this farm. But when Janice and I came to take possession, sight unseen, late in the winter of 1969, the low brooder shed lay wind-flattened on a ridge behind the barn. Nearer the highway stood the two-story house. From where we sat peering out the window of our idling VW bus, the structure looked suitably weathered, its siding having gone so long without paint that the original coat of white was no longer peeling—all that remained of the color was pigment that had leached into the grain. From the highway the house looked gray.

It was surrounded by ridges of walnut and oak; sycamores stood along the banks of the two clear creeks that crossed the acreage, and we'd been told there were blackberry thickets on the hillsides, groves of persimmon and wild plum.

"It really looks like home, doesn't it!" I gushed. "Like the kind of place you call 'the old home place.' "

"Yes!"

Since Janice and I had been gypsies for seven months, we were yearning for a hearth. We had been living in Mexico, pretending to be in exile from Nixon's Amerika, but we had run out of funds and were homesick.

The landlady had offered the farm to us for $20 a month (she knew we were poor artists and would take care of it), and the idea appealed to us—after all, across Amerika, in Tennessee and Taos and northern California, as well as just south of us in deeper Ozark "hollers," droves of young communards were slopping their hogs and making hippie bread with no preservatives. It was okay to relinquish our expatriation if the alternative meant growing our own chemical-free food and practicing recycling.

We had never seen a head of lettuce anywhere but in a grocery, and the idea of fertilized brown eggs was secretly revolting. But that didn't matter, because we had, tucked in the van, maybe with my Alan Watts books, or under our Mexican crockery and woven ponchos, or beside the ubiquitous guitar and stacks of Crosby, Stills and Nash records, my copy of *The Whole Earth Catalog*. I'd just walk about with it in one hand and the right implement in the other and soon we'd be cultivating and weaving and reaping right along with those bucolic utopians down on the Hog Farm.

As we came merrily down the drive, we were able to take in the grounds for the first time. Firewood and trikes, what looked like an old washer. In the yard, a white enamel stove, an unshod '58 Chevy on concrete blocks. Pulling up to the house, we emerged onto a nasty surprise: The yard was littered with old clothing and broken crockery, mismatched ragged tennis shoes, TV dinner tins, soggy magazines, soggy cardboard boxes full of soggy newspapers, nests of coat hangers and two dead dogs. We began to wonder about the wisdom of having rented the place sight unseen.

The dogs had been shot in the head. I presumed they had been executed by the previous tenants, the hillbillies who had been ousted by the landlady for a variety of sins, chief among them being, I suspected, that they were white trash who stood in the way of the property coming under our better care. I had felt guilty that we had displaced them—that they were Joads—but after I saw the yard, I pictured Pa behind the wheel of a jam-packed pickup as he leaned out to holler, "Dag-nabit, Luke, I fergot to shoot the dogs!" the way you'd say, "Catch the lights for me, will you?" Then I felt better: They weren't Joads; they were Snopeses. Their decorative motif was repeated with various embellishments inside the house. One bedroom had been used as a kennel. The seatless toilet was filled to the porcelain rim with festering turds and tobacco juice.

Undaunted, we went to work. For five weeks we scraped, sanded, stained and varnished the floors; we repainted walls and woodwork; lay new linoleum in the kitchen and painted the cabinets. I replumbed some water lines there to use as washer and dryer hook-ups. We put up screens, built a shower for the bathroom, had the septic tank cleaned, replaced broken laterals. We bought a wood-burning stove with chrome fenders and helmet, and I went out with a chain saw and cut deadfall in the woods to burn in it—it was our only source of heat save for the propane cookstove in the kitchen.

I'll say this for Janice and me as a couple—we would have made an excellent team of mules. We both loved to work; we were both compulsive. We were the kind of people who, one day after moving into an apartment, made it look as if we'd been there a year. Janice was petite, a size 5 with dainty, anchorwoman features, but she was a swimmer and dancer and could, like an ant, rearrange a room of furniture by herself and she didn't mind getting dirty. Like me, she was full of nervous energy that needed an outlet. Even after a long day spent working hard, she would, once seated to talk to company, cross one leg over the other then slip the toes of the crossed leg behind the fixed leg's calf, giving the impression her legs were wound up like the two halves of a large rubber band and that if you gave her a big goose she'd go rocketing through the ceiling. For my part, I was always the only person who'd sing "99 Bottles of Beer on the Wall" all the way down to none on high school band trips.

Soon the place was livable. Spring had come, and we opened front and rear doors during the day to enjoy the balmy air, the stillness, the smell of forsythia and redbud, lilac, the aroma of warm wet earth. We'd go tramping through the woods and pastures, and the lines from Dylan Thomas's "Fern Hill" would run like a river through my mind: ". . . and green and golden, I was huntsman, I was herdsman . . ."

With a borrowed tractor, I churned up a patch and planted garden-variety vegetables plus some items I had never heard of, such as "kohlrabi," which made me feel like a benignly mad agronomist. I bought the seeds in a nearby village at a hardware store so old-fashioned they kept everything in barrels. The walls were honeycombed with little drawers and pigeonholes you reached by climbing up on a ladder that moved along a track. Hanging from the ceiling was a hornet's nest big as a basketball. The clerks were all elderly men in spectacles and green eyeshades. (I hold one of them responsible, by the way, for the well-house burning down.)

We built a scarecrow to keep birds away from the to-matoes and the corn, but it wouldn't scare the raccoons, and at least one groundhog relocated his burrow so that he'd be within easy reach of ripe tomatoes, scarecrow notwithstanding. Later that summer we canned tomatoes, peaches and green beans, and made jams and jellies out of our own blackberries and wild plums. We pickled cucumbers and seasoned them with garlic and dill we had grown ourselves.

Oh, this was a good life! We were poor but rich. When the weather got nice, we strung a hammock on the porch, and when friends visited we'd sit on the stoop, drink cheap California wine, and feel self-righteous. When the weather was cold, we'd sit around the stove in the living room and put our damp-socked feet up on the warm chrome fenders.

We had part-time jobs at a small state college nearby, Janice in the theater department and I in English. They didn't pay much, but our overhead was low, and we lived quite happily like tenant farmers on what we could scrounge, happily, that is, until some crisis (usually automotive) depleted our meager resources. We bought no new clothes; we never ate out; and I remember carefully allotting myself a quarter to get a Coke to drink with my brown bag sandwich on days I'd go to town to teach.

Poverty, then, was hip. Uncut hair and ragged jeans signified superior priorities. When I wasn't teaching, gardening, cutting wood or making repairs, I was steadily writing my novel in the attic, where I had remodeled a long, dark triangular space by cutting out and glassing in one of the gables. I made a built-in bench under the windows so that I could look out across the back lot, to the weathered barn, the well-house, the pond and down to the creek. My blue heaven.

It seems extraordinary now, this activity. Never in eight years of marriage had we done such frantic nest-building, plunged ourselves so into the heart of the heart of things by pushing seeds into the ground and tending shoots for later harvesting, engaged in such frantic carpentry and painting that you'd think we were expecting some decidedly singular visit or inspection. True to ourselves, Janice and I never seemed to be working together so much as we were working adjacent to one another in space and time, in tandem but not precisely in unison, each of us concentrating on a separate task, each self-absorbed and determined, mindless as bugs.

We were working up to something Big. We collected stray dogs and cats that had been dumped on the highway.

One day, five months after we had arrived, Janice came back from a doctor's appointment, walked into my study and said, "Well, I'm pregnant." She wore a comedienne's wry little moue that told me she wasn't sure how to react. After I heard "pregnant" I looked pretty closely to see how she felt so I could figure out how *I* felt. She looked scared but excited; it was as if she'd just heard she'd been accepted by a club she'd wanted to get into but whose initiation required jumping from an airplane.

While I was watching Janice, she was waiting for me to respond.

"Really? Huh!" I reacted finally, as if to news of an interesting development overseas. I know now it was inadequate; I can say now for sure what I was *supposed* to feel and do—yell "Wonderful!" and grab her in my arms and kiss her. But I didn't know what to express either, and mostly I felt scared the way she did. I've always absorbed news slowly, and I have to walk around it several times, sniffing at it, before I locate my true response.

Even had I felt like whooping with joy I wouldn't have because I wasn't sure what Janice felt. I wouldn't have wanted to be the only person whooping. And she wasn't about to do it first, for the same reason. Each was waiting to discover what the other felt before committing to a position. These were the automatic, delicate negotiations between two people accustomed to hiding their feelings from each other.

"How'd it happen?" I meant, considering that she had been taking birth control pills for eight years and hadn't gotten pregnant, why now? I didn't intend any reproach, but in retrospect I can see how, from the point of view of a just-pregnant woman who might want to hear some whooping, my question was ill-considered.

"I guess when I forgot to take my pill a couple of days in a row two months ago and tripled up it messed up my cycle." She sounded apologetic.

"Huh!" I said. "What do you think we should do?"

"I don't know. What do you think we should do?"

"I don't know."

For many years after—until the moment I wrote about it—I believed that this was the accidental result of Janice's inattention to detail. Now I'm convinced that it was an intentional, perhaps unconscious act: After eight years, you don't suddenly forget to take birth control pills unless you're secretly hoping for the consequences. Her biological clock was ticking.

So was mine. Pushing thirty, I was feeling the child-lessness that afflicts monks. But being dutiful, open-minded liberals, we discussed abortion first. We had to be realistic. Here I was banging away at my novel and enduring poverty for the sake of art, working part-time; Janice wasn't fully employed, either, and wasn't getting a chance to do what she wanted—be a theatrical director, if not on Broadway, at least in some clouty regional center. Her career was important; she was a first-generation feminist who had already gone through three copies of *The Feminine Mystique* simply because she kept giving them away to her friends.

We scarcely had a penny that wasn't spent before it passed into our hands. How could we afford a child? How could we manage, living out of town on a farm, to work part-time in town if someone had to be here with the baby? We had no medical insurance to boot.

We discussed the practical questions long into the night and reached no conclusion.

But we never discussed a more important consideration: Was our marriage solid enough to survive this? We had married impetuously while still in college, both on the rebound. We were in a hurry and didn't really know each other. This produced several rocky years in succession. During our third year of marriage, we had separated while Janice sought greener pastures, but I had coaxed, cajoled and brow-beaten her to come back to me. Our fourth and fifth years had been a healing time, our sixth we'd spent in Mexico as boon companions, helpmates, lovers and friends—and the time we'd spent so far on the farm convinced me that our marriage was getting stronger as each year went by.

Now we had mutual interests, passions and convictions; we got angry together about the same injustices. We had mutual friends and enemies. We were good allies and supported one another in our departmental struggles as teachers or in arguments on issues at parties. We had a large parcel of common history to solidify us, a common background. We had hammered out a mutual respect and a sense of brotherhood; we had a smoothly running partnership, with occasional gusts of passion. This bond now seemed a strong enough glue to bear the strain of whatever came, and I also felt that any marriage too weak to bear the weight of children wasn't worth having anyway.

I began making offhand comments designed to declare my new positive position. Sometimes they were pitifully bald—a discussion of governmental programs for the poor might inspire something like "Lots of poor people have children, and they survive it quite nicely and enjoy life." Janice still balked. I think she wanted me to talk her into this so she would know where I stood. So one night I pushed us off the fence. I kept grinning and joking abut "little tykes" and "patter of tiny feet," trying to josh her into agreement. I made her know that I did, indeed, want a child. I felt that at heart she wanted one too, though later on I worried that I had merely bullied her into agreement the way I had pushed us to attend our particular graduate school and then dragged us to our first jobs in Missouri; the way I had taken us to Mexico then back to this farm; the way, I feared, I had twisted her arm to come back to me.

Then she seemed content to play the expectant mother. Pregnant, she was never more healthy, she said. She felt wonderful. Her migraines vanished. On Fridays she was weighed by our obstetrician's nurse, who frowned if she gained more than the allotted poundage, so she would gorge on weekends then slack off until the following Thursday before weigh-in. Only one snapshot exists of her pregnant: She's standing beside a neighbor's garden wearing a brown knee-length smock, a petite woman with a tummy big as a basketball. (This was the photograph she least liked.)

During one weekly visit, Janice's doctor thought he heard two fetal heartbeats. For a week we were awestruck with the possibility that our first child would be two children, but when the doctor checked again the following week he heard only one heartbeat. We pored over Dr. Spock and scrounged about for a crib and bedding and clothing; we worried, for the first time, about the distance we lived from town.

Janice was in labor about eight hours; the nurses doped her up and I held her hand for a while, but when they wheeled her off to deliver, I was led to the waiting room; none of that natural childbirth stuff for me. Several other people—surprisingly, not all of them men—were already there. You'd have thought it was a group from Schick practicing aversion therapy with cigarettes. I pitched in by lighting up my pipe. I quickly picked out the expectant fathers and identified with them: The vets were yawning and snoozing, while we rookies were all zombie-eyed and chatty, lounging about like a dismissed platoon waiting to be called back into formation.

My pipe was a new affectation. It probably looked foolish, but it made me feel mature. My father smoked a pipe. Being on the brink of fatherhood, I considered the fathering I had had myself. I thought about how my father taught me to stand when ladies enter a room and how to handle hammers, saws and oars, and once, at age twelve, I saw him rescue a drowning man—a father—from a river and walk away without giving anyone his name. A hero. When I was growing up, he took me to his Presbyterian church. While I had never heard him utter a single Biblical quotation, I had likewise never heard him curse except if, say, he accidentally put hammer head to fingernail ("Damn!"), and his usual mode of discourse was the witty one-liner.

I thought about how he seldom talked about himself or passed on any lore from his own boyhood, though I did know that he had studied for a year at Vanderbilt during the Depression and hoped to be a doctor (he didn't make it); he made money by tramping through the Smokies selling Bibles, a thrifty, hard-working, Scots-Irish follower of Knox and Calvin. He was a person with considerable reserve—people call him a good listener—and whatever

24

problems he may have had growing up, or later at work, or whatever difficulties he had living with my mother (his childhood sweetheart), or us, he never talked about. He got ulcers instead. We never went fishing or hunting together—we were never "just the boys"—but the family went camping frequently, and when I went out for football in the ninth grade, he'd always sit in the bleachers on Saturday afternoons to watch me sit on the bench.

Whenever I heard the word "gentleman," I thought of my father. It seemed a good standard to aspire to. I enjoyed thinking that he had passed on his attributes. As for his shortcomings, well, I was arrogant enough to imagine that whatever they had been, when it came to me and my own son, I could fill in the gaps with my new, improved version of our particular set of genes.

Now and then a nun with a beatific grin stuck her head in the room and scanned our faces tantalizingly, milking the suspense like a beauty-pageant m.c. We all craned forward, holding our breath. Oh, is it me? Is it me? The man called would then go out with a smile.

At last, she sang out, "Oh, Mr. Smith," with an odd lilt to her voice. *Have we got a surprise for you!* I hardly registered that she had made her announcement to me with a little extra oomph. I followed her into the hall; she strode swiftly ahead toward the recovery room, the hem of her long habit swaying like a broom and keeping me at a distance.

"And what did you want, Mr. Smith?"

"What did I want?" I couldn't understand her question. A baby, a normal baby, that's what I had wanted.

"Did you want a boy or a girl?"

She was moving quickly, and I had to scurry up to the perimeter of her habit—it was like trying to dance in the

*25*

Fifties with girls who wore crinoline slips—and peer around her chubby cheek to watch her mouth. She moved as if on wheels.

"Well, either, I guess."

"That's good," she said merrily.

That's good? Why was that good? If it weren't for her smirk, I'd have been terrified.

"What'd I get?"

"What you wanted." She snickered, very pleased with herself.

Oh, my God! Are we talking hermaphrodites here?

"What do you—"

"A boy and a girl, Mr. Smith." Then she turned to beam at me. "Twins! And they're both doing fine, got all their parts."

Oh, those sneaky devils! One hiding his or her heartbeat behind the other's! They had managed to lie close together until the last—actually penultimate—moment, when Nicole came out. Four minutes later, to everyone's surprise, even the doctor's, out popped Keith.

I leaned against the wall outside the recovery room to let this news sink in. It sank to the bottom. I wasn't happy. But I also wasn't sad, or angry. I felt the anxiety that comes from a loss of control.

I'd always had an intense need to dominate my life, had always felt up to it and thought I had done a fairly good job so far, my poverty notwithstanding. But now I felt hopelessly inadequate. It was as if I had spent months preparing for the most important examination of my life only to discover upon taking the test that half of it covered material I had not known to study.

Twins? *Two* infants?

This meant double everything—cribs, diaper sets, bottles, strollers, car seats, kangaroo carriers, high chairs, wash basins, blankets, cases of formula, packages of safety pins and nightshirts (blue and pink), booties and pj's and sleepers and mobiles and pacifiers . . . We had prepared for one, carefully, borrowing and buying and depending on friends and relatives to help. Capriciously, nature had given us not a child but an emergency.

We had no medical insurance and had scraped through the wood at the bottom of the barrel to pay for one delivery. Would the hospital and the doctors charge double?

I hadn't the foggiest notion of how to care for one, let alone two babies.

Then, too, twinness was an oddity. The concept had always seemed remote, a slightly freakish thing that happened to others. To my knowledge, neither family had any history of it (oh, the things you're never told until after the fact). I had known a set of fraternal twins in high school—Danny and Danielle. They were both hulking and homely and wore similar eyeglasses; they looked alike except that Danielle had longer hair and her mustache wasn't as flourishing.

Being the father of twins was not the same as being the father of one or two children; it put me in another category altogether, one I had never considered. It somehow diminished my importance, the way the parents of an idiot savant must feel when the TV crews come to film the little monkey as he flawlessly rips through the Warsaw Concerto on the family upright. I had a hankering after fame, but the extra attention I'd get for this wasn't any of my doing.

These were stupid thoughts, really. And selfish. I was too stunned to think more lofty ones. But slowly, my natural optimism made me count my blessings. At least we would be able to use both of the names we had spent so many hours worrying over. I had been given the opportunity to have an Experience of long duration, a parental trial by fire, and I would be larger for having had this happen to me, would learn doubly what being a parent meant.

More importantly, these children had "all their parts," as the nun had so quaintly put it. No stillbirth, Down's syndrome, deformities, no tiny brain squashed by an impatient doctor's forceps—every expectant parent's nightmare.

And Janice, how was she?

I pushed through the door to the recovery room. She was struggling to sit up in bed, clad in a wrinkled, bile-green hospital smock. She was still groggy, her face mottled and distorted as if she had given birth to herself.

I took her hand. "Well, well!" I said, grinning. Now it was my turn to play the nun's trick.

But she had already heard something. She looked at me, glassy-eyed, an odd half-smile on her lips.

"Is it true? There's two?"

I nodded, still grinning moronically. I was not putting on a Happy Face; I was trying to encourage her to feel as I did, that we were the objects of some genuinely witty and inventive cosmic prank.

"Oh, I'm sorry!" she blurted out.

She's *sorry?* She thinks this is her *fault?*

"Hey, it's okay!" I said.

I should have said "I love you," but I wasn't that kind of guy, then.

Later I stood at the glass wall with other fellows I recognized from the waiting room. We were all lined up, as if at the bay window of an underground aquarium, watching for the creatures we had spawned to come swimming out of the evolutionary murk. Beside me, a young man in overalls kept pointing out his offspring to his companion, saying "Ten pounds, ten pounds!" as if he had landed a Guinness-record bass. I was tempted to add the weight of my tadpoles and say something like, "Fourteen pounds, ten ounces!" but I hadn't yet located in the heaving jumble of my various emotions sufficient masculine pride to compete with him.

A sea cow in white polyester waved a flipper over two nearby bassinets, and I stood tip-toe to see over their rims. Who was who? Two red worms, squirming in their shells, sea-critters, their salty blood still evident in the membrane and tissue that covered their bones. I was dumbstruck. This is how life begins.

Had I been so ugly and . . . well, primordial? Had my own parents shook at the terror of this responsibility? I knew there were people who *tried* to have children, people—saints!—who had four and adopted others, people who had begun their married lives with little else in mind but to be fruitful and multiply. There were perhaps even people whose love for each other was so overpowering and magnificent that their children rose like bread dough from that yeast.

Janice had said "I'm sorry" as if expecting me to be angry. It was the most unguarded and heartfelt expression of her feelings that I'd ever heard her utter. It still is. I wasn't the slightest bit angry. But I had been handed a harder job than I had bargained for; I was prepared to grit my teeth and take on the challenge, but oh, was I scared! We had doubled in size and paradoxically seemed outnumbered. We needed to be fully adults all at once; these humans to whom we had been assigned were helpless, and their greatest need played to our greatest insufficiency and ignorance. And for a person full of equivocation and contradiction, there could be no terror worse than having options closed out. It might bring relief from making choices, but it also meant that something more powerful than I controlled my life.

I had no idea that they would become bona fide people, with identifiable personalities, to whom I could relate as one person to another. Or that people learn to parent by practicing it on their children, by getting on-the-job training.

I didn't have any idea of how profoundly interesting they would become, that not even my writing could be as much fun or as richly entertaining as fathering. Or as difficult.

I had no idea that they would be so easy to fall in love with. They did not constitute the threat of desertion that full-grown humans could present by announcing out of the blue that they were leaving you. They would not withdraw their love. They had no consciousness of me except through my hands and voice and face and my pulse and my heartbeat as I held them and talked nonsense. They would not embarrass me by repeating what I said, nor would they refuse to take anything of myself I gave them. Their commitment to me would be lifelong; even when they hated me they would continue to love me.

Holding them, wiping their messy bums, pinning their diapers, marveling at how their grapefruit-sized heads just fit the palm of one hand and their tiny buttocks the palm of the other, I felt a rush of freedom: Here were persons who could never choose *not* to love me. I had been given, unsolicited, an instant fan club.

But there was work to do. Fortunately, we had help. Friends celebrated our bounty by appearing with appliances and clothing and blankets and cases of formula, an extra crib, another stroller, another high chair. Our house had the air of a Red Cross gathering center, and you'd have thought a tornado had ripped off the roof. Janice's mother came to stay and seemed wholly nonplussed. Janice and I darted frantically from the pages of Dr. Spock to the cribs, where the babes would throw us into spasms of anxiety by doing something new, and since they were utterly novel to us, anything they did—gurgling, babbling, crapping and pissing, winking, coughing or waving their tiny limbs—was strange and seemed to require a response. Janice's mother had to teach us that just because our babies were doing something, it did not necessarily mean that we had to do something back. Sometimes parenting was a spectator sport.

The twins' instinct for self-preservation encouraged them to wake in shifts at night, so that Janice and I could trade off, but they came at it differently. Keith awoke to his feeding times with an angry howl—he's still, like me, very cross before being fed—and when you picked him up and held him to give him his bottle, he squirmed and struggled, as if to get free of your clutches. His head was shaped like a hot-air balloon; his hair was darkish and thin, and he had bags under his eyes. He was colicky and needed a variation on the standard formula. But Nicole was placid and self-contained, and sometimes when my Pavlovian response would awaken me for her feeding, I'd walk into their room to find her already awake and watchful. When she cried, she sounded uncomfortable or unhappy, but hardly ever angry. She had a moon-shaped face and, soon, a jumble of yellow curls.

Their bodies were amazing. Everything was so, so *miniature!* And such precision of detail on these little replicas! The roseate curls of their delicate ear-flesh had the awe-inspiring conformation of sea shells; their fingers, no longer than a joint of my own, had knuckles like minute raisins and nails the size and shape of scales on a minnow's hide. Their biceps and thighs were cartoonishly rounded, like little pink sausages, and their hairless pubes and balls were comical and alien. Shortly after they came home, their skin tone went from a mottled red to a smooth and delicate pink, and they no longer looked torn from the womb. Their drool and spittle was clear as distilled water, and even their runny green crap seemed like an innocuous paste. (That's not to say it didn't stink.)

When I lifted them, their density and weight surprised me; their passivity made me feel clumsy and anxious, like Gulliver among the Liliputians.

*You might accidentally drop one. Or maybe you'll try to feed one too quickly and they'll choke. Or in the night Sudden Crib Death syndrome could drift through a partially opened window and infect them. And, speaking of open windows, check Spock, what's he say about babies and air from outside—"Enthusiasm for Fresh Air Varies Greatly in Different Parts of the Country, and in Different Personality Types"—Thanks a lot, Doctor! For nothing! And for Christ's sake we might not know it now, but one might be brain-damaged even as we whisper in the dark, see what you-know-who says the signs are, they're already supposed to be moving this or that, and what's this rash that looks like a fungus from outer space, and—oh, my God! this is the worst!—they're screaming bloody murder and they've just been fed and changed and burped so what in the world could it be, could either be a gas pain or they're pissed off or they need an emergency appendectomy!*

*Be calm, be calm! Here, let me croon you to sleep with a lullaby from Spock:* "Most of us are so inexperienced when we start with our first baby that we are anxious about everything: his hiccups, his temperature, his weight, his breathing. His first fall—"

*Fall?!*

"—frightens us and overwhelms us with guilt. When he has his first nose cold, it seems like a major illness."

*So my anxiety is normal, is it? I'm overreacting, am I?*

*Yes, and perfectly healthy. Everybody does it.*

*But that doesn't mean that there couldn't be some emergency-type situation that justified my anxiety!*

*Easy, there!* "Our overconcern shows in our faces, our voices, the speed with which we respond to his cry. Some of this anxiety rubs off on him—"

*Oh great! I'm not supposed to be anxious because it rubs off, but on the other hand my anxiety is perfectly natural? Thanks a lot, Doctor, for nothing!*

*Now, now. Listen:* "Our fears about his physical safety usually tone down as the months go by. The same can't be said of our anxieties about his behavior and about our ability to control it. These worries become worse during the second—"

*Hold it! If this is going to get harder, I don't want to hear about it beforehand!*

At the end of their first week, they were still living. A photographer from the weekly newspaper in the village came to take a picture of Janice with the two babies for Mother's Day. In the yard, Janice knelt in the grass and laid the twins along the inside of her forearms, a gardener showing off prize-winning pumpkins. In the picture that appeared on the front page, she is grinning, grinning, grinning. I felt left out.

Summer came, then fall. They could hold their heads up; they could turn over in their cribs unassisted, then came sitting up, reaching up to grasp the mobiles and trapeze contraptions hanging over their heads. Once they got the hang of it, they were all motion. They crawled and lifted themselves up in their cribs, and they'd stand with their arms hooked over the sides like sailors watching the shore slip by. They'd bang their rattles on the crib bars, chortle at one another and sling their pacifiers into the dining room. I quickly lost my fear of hurting them or dropping them: Putting my hands around their waists, I'd lift them over my head and gently swing them around, playing airplane; I'd pitch them up so that they'd fly out of my hands and flail their arms and hold their breaths and make their eyes grow round with surprise and apprehension, and then, when I'd catch them on the way down and laugh, they'd shriek with delight.

By the next spring, we put them in backpacks with canvas seats and set off tramping through our pastures. They liked motion, being on the move (and who doesn't?), and every snapshot of them riding like papooses shows them smiling. Put onto the carpet in their room and left to their own devices, they'd tug open their drawers and drag out their clothes. I had to put a hinged gate on their door to keep them from crawling into the house. Soon we needed locks on all the cabinets, and soon every place became accessible. You set them on the living room floor and gave them a big ball to fool with, got up to get coffee from the kitchen, and when you returned to the living room they were climbing on the bookcases. I had fun being their climbing tree; they'd crawl up the trunks of my legs, sit on the branches of my outstretched arms, perch on my neck, and survey the world from way up there. I enjoyed their squirming weight, their heft, their baby-powder smell, and when they were up in their climbing tree, I'd baste their exposed flesh with my nose and sniff them up. They were delicious.

I discovered I had a capacity for tenderness that I had left behind in childhood when I last had a pet I had adored. Keith and Nicole made me mushy and silly; just to look at them made heat surge up and down my spine and the hair prickle on my neck. These hot flashes of sticky love felt distinctly different with each. With Nicole, it was more protective, more gentle; with Keith, I wanted to clap his back and scruff up his hair, punch him on the arm. Feeling the rush, the high, I uttered odd sounds, collections of syllables that inexplicitly always contained the vowels "oo" or rhymed with them (as in "gitchy-goo boo-boo"); they made me say things that I wouldn't be caught dead saying to any other human.

Being a father played on different aspects of my personality, the way an organist produces different interpretations of the same music by altering the stops. It quadrupled the number of my frustrations, and likewise increased my patience. I learned to relish small pauses in the chaotic tumble of ceaseless activity. Having my hands wrist-deep in baby-crap subdued the demands of my ego that I be seen as a dignified creature. It was humbling. I was but a valet and maid to infant royalty, and they, the young, were all that mattered. Nature had ceased to care about my welfare and had instead entirely bent my life to this higher purpose. This in turn made me feel like a glorious martyr; I was far superior to those poor selfish single shmucks who dreamed that a better life meant bigger toys and having no strings attached. I was becoming a "better" person for being a father. Parenthood was making me as smug as a small-town Baptist preacher.

But with winter life became more difficult. The house was drafty; the wood-stove in the living room had been sufficient for pioneering hippies, but with two crawling infants more heat was needed. I bought an old propane space heater cheap, but since it wasn't vented I couldn't leave it on at night. During the day we fretted that one of the children would get burned, although except when they were being bathed or changed, Keith and Nicole lived in layers of soggy clothing. They had trouble sleeping because their nostrils clogged with snot, and you'd spend half a night teaching them to blow their noses.

After a heavy snow, the stretch of two-rut road to the highway was impassable—whereas the previous winter this always had given me a curious elation (being snowed-in was oddly festive), now we couldn't secure supplies and we'd be stuck in an emergency. When the weather was bitter cold, we couldn't relieve our cabin fever by leaving, and we felt trapped. Then our infants' helplessness paradoxically made them omnipotent, and I chafed at how they tyrannized us. They seemed absolutely unreasonable, unrelentingly demanding. They had no qualms about waking us up in the middle of the night and screaming at us even when we were wandering like zombies in REM sleepland; they didn't care the slightest if we were reading a book or were in the middle of eating a meal we had spent thirty minutes preparing—when they wanted something, they wanted it instantly. They did not allow us to make plans without first making very elaborate arrangements for their welfare. They came first, always, and we couldn't even accuse them of selfishness or prick them with guilt. They couldn't put on their own socks or tie their shoes or wipe their asses or get themselves something to eat—and Good Lord, wouldn't they ever learn to blow their own noses!

In February the temperature plummeted below zero for several days. The pipes in the well-house froze, shutting off our water supply. We broke the ice in the pond and dipped our wash water up in buckets for days, and hauled in drinking water from town. We stank like goats. We put the dirty dishes and diapers out on the back porch. At the village hardware store, one of the elderly clerks told me that he had unthawed frozen pipes by wrapping them in kerosene-soaked rags which he'd then ignited. It sounded okay to me, but then I once fell for a snipe hunt. The interior walls of the well-house were covered with shredding plywood, and no sooner had I stepped back after lighting the rags than the flames hopped nimbly onto the peeling siding. Then I couldn't do anything but stand outside and watch the old structure go awash with flames. I thought of calling the fire department, but there was none. I thought of using a hose and dousing the fire, but there was no water. It gave me a peculiar but powerful sense of helplessness, the way it took this accident so long to finish itself while I stood by dancing, looking frantically for a partner. It was like having a car wreck in slow motion. My helplessness scared me. I was responsible for so many things now.

So when the next winter came, it was time to leave the farm. I remember, though, an afternoon in October, just after we had made the hard decision to leave.

I'm lying in the hammock on the porch, with Nicole zipped up in her pink flannel jumpsuit, breathing evenly in sleep in the crook of my arm next to my ribs. Strong sunshine, yellow light streaming through the branches of the high white-barked sycamores along the creek that runs a stone's throw from the porch. They've got their knobby knees in that cold water, those old men sycamores, and their large hand-shaped leaves are turning yellow and brown on their edges. I can see this from where I lie; my eyes are in the shade, but my moccasins are soaking up the sunlight and warming my feet. I'm wearing an old flannel shirt, and as I sway slightly in the hammock, pushed, it seems, by the locomotion of our own slow breathing, I can feel the coolness penetrate my back, making a delicious contrast against the heat of the sunlight creeping up my legs from my shins, so that as the moments slide by I'm being very slowly immersed in a bath of warm light.

The day is balmy, but the air hints of restlessness. Now and then a fitful huff of wind sends a stiff leaf skittering across the concrete porch, rattles a web of leaves caught in the crooks of the firewood I cut and stacked by the front door. Keith is sleeping, Janice is out running errands, so no sound comes through the screen door from inside, but I can smell, very faintly, the aroma of burning wood from the coals dying in the bottom of the stove. Last night was chilly, as was the morning, so we had the fire going, but the day has grown warmer as it has gone on, like a recuperating patient feeling a midday strength. Against my left flank I can feel this child, my daughter, giving off heat, her slight breath not audible but visible in the rise and fall of her chest. Below her blonde hair, the skin on her forehead and temples is pale, and through it I see a network of fine blue veins.

This morning I wrote three pages on my novel, replaced a faulty valve in the washing machine and split firewood with an axe and a wedge. I hung clumps of red and yellow onions from the rafters of the shed with strings. Now no one or no thing calls me or waits; I'm pleasantly caught in the web of a lull. I can feel my blood slowly spurting through my veins. Over the ridge to the east, somebody is working on a tree with an axe; I hear a steady tap of the steel on the wood, then a rest, then the tapping again.

Under this tranquillity a slow pulse thrums in plant cells, water from the creek oozes into the tissue of the sycamore roots, and if I walk down past the blackened well-house hulk and to the water I might see, say, a snake with the head of a frog protruding from its distended mouth. Last night I heard the yowling of the old battered tomcat from the barn, where he stops by periodically on his sojourns throughout the countryside to give our female tabby a shake by the nape of her neck and to inject his jism into her womb. Mounted dragonflies reproduce in dizzy flight. Walking about aimlessly, I can stumble onto eggs and carcasses and husks that demonstrate transformations gone full cycle; there will be skeletons turning chalk-white from the weather, all flesh stripped from the bones by ants and minute organisms. Down by the water, quiet feasts occur nightly: A raccoon and her cubs root under submerged rocks for crawfish and snag slow minnows with their sharp claws. A cow with aching, bulbous sides stands on the hillside grinding grass with her molars; patiently she allows herself to be used as a hide-bound shell for growing other cows.

*Now I'm part of this grand cycle,* I think.

It occurs to me, on the eve of leaving, that the themes for these last two years have been fecundity and transformation. I shed skins like the snakes I saw on the rocky limestone hillsides. I had come to the farm an old young man but would leave it a young old man. I had come with a batch of messy sketches and would leave with a novel that would soon be published. I had come having been no closer to a garden than a supermarket and would leave having tilled the soil, sown the seed and made the harvest; having preserved, canned and stored the crop for the winter. I'd learned to make jam and jelly and pickles; I'd learned plumbing and propane and wiring and roofing; I'd learned to tell an oak from a maple, a cardinal from a sparrow.

I had come as a son but would leave as a father.

# TWO

# "Green Eggs and Ham"

Dr. Spock was right. Our fears about our toddlers' physical safety toned down as the months went by, but not "our anxieties about his behavior and our ability to control it. The worries become worse the second year, when a baby ceases to be just a cute and compliant doll."

Nothing puts you smack up against the shortcomings of your character more than being a parent, and my anger and frustration popped up to live alongside me like an unwanted relative. *I was not cut out for this,* I began to think. They flung their food from their high chairs and smeared their faces with it; they crapped in their pants and painted the walls with their dung; when we put something down on the coffee table (book, car keys, wallet) it would be chewed up, spat on, stomped on, dragged off, torn apart or dipped in shit in seconds flat. We put anything dangerous (mouth-sized) or valuable inside cabinets or up on shelves above neck-high to an adult. I was living in a weird soup with my head just above the surface, where order lay like a very thin stratum of oxygen in a room filling up with

water; below my shoulders were half-human, half-animal
critters who crawled and ran about, and the "vegetables"
in this soup were their balls and trucks and bottles and
pacifiers and security blankets and rattles and shoes and
socks and broken-backed books by Dr. Seuss. I felt as if
I were drowning in a sea of displaced objects. I knew that
my craving for order was inappropriate for our situation,
but I couldn't seem to set it aside for when it would be
sensible. I could neither ignore my need for order nor
spend the time it took to appease it. So I got angry. My
jaw was permanently clenched.

We had moved into town within blocks of the campus
and necessary services, but even so we were painfully aware
of restrictions on our personal freedom. Since we had no
medical insurance, we had relied on scraps of savings for
emergencies; we had little money for baby-sitters, and in
two years we ate out only on one occasion, the time we
decided to take the kids as a learning experience—theirs,
not ours. If, in our desperation to go somewhere stimu-
lating, we decided to attend a party, we'd spend days jock-
eying to find a free sitter.

Within our home the perimeter of our personal freedom
collapsed like a balloon. Any space for writing or reading
required clearing away first. Janice and I had no time together except between midnight and six, when we were
too exhausted to do anything but drop to sleep before
being awakened by a child who needed a nose blown or
wet diapers changed. During the day, one of us stayed
home while the other was out working or shopping. Before
having my children, I wondered what housewives did with
the spare time they had between feedings, but I soon learned
that when the kids were awake they required vigilance—
once Keith crawled up and over our backyard fence and
was found strolling in diapers down a sidewalk a block

away. When they were sleeping I'd get a respite, but I'd never know if it would be for three minutes or three hours. Putting them down to nap, I'd settle in with a book and notepad only to be interrupted every five minutes. Giving up and deciding that I might as well fold clothes or put away dishes, I'd find that they had fallen mysteriously silent. Young children abhor a parent's self-absorption the way nature abhors a vacuum; they had a diabolically accurate instinct for knowing precisely when I needed my own mind, and as soon as my attention turned inward it set off an alarm in them.

I wish I could say I accepted my lot with grace. At times I did, but having a life of nothing but endless chores made me whine and grumble. I was working hard to bring in income, and I was working hard at being a writer. I grew up in cowboy country in a traditional household, though my mother did work and I did see my father scrub a bathroom floor. Part of me insisted that bringing up babies was women's work. Another part said writers were supposed to be having intelligent conversation in salons or pubs rather than trying to dress a balky, sullen child for an outing through the snow to the supermarket, an outing fated to be torture for both.

But my consciousness was being raised. My traditional side also held that the male was supposed to *support* his wife, but having failed that, I felt it only fair that if Janice had to assume part of that duty, then I should accept an equal share in raising the children.

We both claimed an equal share in the role of martyrs. It's one of the few rewards for sacrificing your sleep, your energy, your time and all your available income on little humans who can't understand if you complain, who can't thank you. We whined in public; we were contemptuous and envious of singles; if a childless couple mentioned that they were planning a weekend getaway, we might say, sarcastically, "Well, it must be nice . . ." We let people know that we were downtrodden; we wanted them to feel guilty about having no responsibilities. We felt superior in our martyrdom just as we felt straight-jacketed in the conditions that caused it.

*Oh, now, be serious! Didn't it all seem worth it sometimes? Didn't you love them? Weren't they ever, well, so cute they tickled you pink? Weren't you an infant once and somebody had to do this for you? It's called life, for God's sake! Your babies never spent an hour in the hospital after they were born, and they required no task or chore that wasn't simply the ordinary effort of bringing up a normal child. You were poor, you say? You never missed a meal, did you? You always had twenty times your share, speaking globally, of all the hot water and electricity and housing you really needed, and not a one of you ever had to wear a rag. Do you seriously think your life was so difficult? Grow up!*

Yes, of course we loved them. And, sure, we took pleasure where we could find it. Their first step? Their first words? One night when Keith was about two and a half, he woke us up crying. We went to see about him and he was curled in a ball, gripping his stomach. We took him into the bathroom, stood him upright and leaned him over the commode. He vomited profusely. He looked down into the toilet, then he turned back to us, in awe of what he had done, and uttered his first complete sentence: "I throw up." We laughed. *Vomito, ergo sum,* I thought. I puke, therefore I am. A perfect little existentialist!

And I never felt so big and strong and grown-up as when one was riding on my shoulders delighted to be up so high or riding on my back, playing horsie. I never felt so loved or needed as when they would run to greet me as I came home, wrapping their limbs around my legs, begging to ride on my shoes.

*If you had it to do over, would you?*

When Ann Landers published her famous poll showing that seventy percent of parents responding said they would *not* do it over, I knew, really, that I wasn't among them. To utter that dark wish of undoing would be to wish them dead, or unborn. I didn't regret giving them life. But when they were six months old, I yearned for when they would be a year old; when they were in their "terrible twos" I wanted them to be three, and at three I wanted them to be four or five. So I kept wishing their lives away in increments, ignoring the present, living in the future when it seemed things would be easier. It *was* like killing them, but with a slow-working poison.

I would do it over, but I had disappointed myself. When the children were born, I'd daydreamed about how they would be reading *The Odyssey* by age five, how they would always be clean and well-behaved in public, how I'd teach them to catch a ball, build a house, name the parts of an orchestra. I'd never let them eat fast-food crap with preservatives. From me they'd learn to treat all humans as equals regardless of race, color, creed or make of automobile. Now, barely three years later, despite my grand intentions, I was a bare-minimum parent. It took every ounce of psychic and physical energy we had to feed, dress, bathe, instruct and discipline them, to shop and house clean, to say nothing of earning an income. Theirs was a People Express flight through childhood in which it seemed no time was left for dallying or having fun with us.

Perhaps my need to make a coherent statement here distorts the picture (it couldn't have been that grim, could it?), but in looking back I can't help but conclude that these children were born to young adults who were financially, psychologically and emotionally unprepared for what it would take to raise them and who never fully reconciled themselves to the task. I had always believed that I did most things well, but here was a job—the most important I ever had—at which I was clearly only mediocre. A "C" had always been a galling grade to me.

Was this normal? I wondered.

And was my anger normal?

They could make me furious. Their behavior was dreadful. In the supermarket I'd set Keith in the cart (I avoided taking both to the grocery at once); his bright little eyes would scan the colorful shelves and his arms would reach out for things. He'd wail if he didn't get them. Or he would want to get out of the cart so he could walk by himself. If I insisted that he hold my hand, he'd go limp in the aisle. To anyone who has never experienced a howling sit-down strike by a two- or three-year-old in a crowded supermarket, I say you've never known real humiliation. You understand how Gandhi won India. Veteran mothers in the crowd will grin in sympathy, but most of the spectators feel that if this child is a monster it's *your* fault.

The kid instinctively knows that here in public you cannot grab his ears, knock his forehead against yours and scream in his face, "Shut the fuck up!" I couldn't do it anyway, but I have seen mothers who apparently felt no such compunction. Once, coming out of a mall, I passed a mother who was trying to make a very balky boy stand and walk. She was pulling up on one of his arms, from which his entire weight was passively, obstinately dangling, and she hissed, "You stand up right now or I'll rip off your balls!"

At home, I reread chapters of Spock entitled "The Aggressive Child" (yes, I have one of those) and "The Daw-

dler" (got one of those too), "The Whiner," "The Poor
Eater," plus "Bet-Wetting" and "Bedtime Problems Around
the Age of Two." They were all pertinent. At least my
children were so normal that their behavior problems had
been neatly codified. I had one bed-wetter who liked to
punch us in the stomach and one whiner who could take
three hours to eat a bowl of oatmeal and who came awake
only when put to bed. Like Dr. Seuss's famous character,
neither one liked "green eggs and ham," and when they
were in the wrong mood, all food fell into that category.

I felt overwhelmed. I felt impotent. Impatience rose in
me like heartburn. Dr. Spock insinuated that corporal punishment is an admission of failure on the parent's part,
failure of the moral imagination, if you will; indeed, all
punishment "is the substitute, emergency method when
the regular system of discipline breaks down." Discipline
was required because we were not patient, loving, understanding or sensible enough to follow a program of "positive verbal requests and prohibitions," such as: "Remember,
you mustn't change the phonograph records—that's Mother's job."

We had no training in handling children other than having *been* children. Janice was the baby of her family. I was
the older child, but could not recall how my younger brother
was raised. My mother yelled and slapped me on the nog-
gin; my father was quiet, but once I was old enough he
used a belt. (To this day I would still obey their reasonable
requests and bear them no grudges.)

But we were also children of the Sixties, and we believed
that to spare the rod was to spare the child. If, as a last
resort, I spanked them, it sometimes got results, sometimes not. But, I'm sorry to say, spanking them made me
feel better; if I refrained from it when it seemed called
for, then for hours, even days, I'd be a little angry, the

way you can be a little fluish but not so sick you have to take to bed. Then I'd take it out on them in little ways, pick or fuss at them for small infractions and be a miser with my love. Spanking them, I purged my anger, and we could go about our business with a fresh start. I'm not advocating this method—even then I knew it's a bad idea to strike a child because it makes you feel better.

Sometimes I'd be so furious that I would clench my fists, leap up and down and bite my knuckles, or I would put my face within a millimeter of theirs and scream bloody murder. If having children had magnified my tenderness, it now, as time went on, pulled out still different stops to get dark tones, an angry slash of purple melody. If I had never known I could love so fiercely, now I was learning I could feel an almost uncontrollable rage.

The time is late fall of 1972. We're renting an old frame two-story house in badly deteriorated condition near the campus. It is spacious, but we have very little furniture; many rooms contain only packing boxes, making us feel as if we're living in a warehouse. High ceilings make the place very hard and very expensive to heat; the old wallpaper in the rooms downstairs is peeling away, and the plumbing upstairs leaks through the ceiling and stains the walls in the rooms below.

Nevertheless, we've struggled to make the public areas of it look homey. The dining room contains our one table and chairs—oak, which I refinished—and we've hung pictures on the walls. The living room has a sofa, a rocking chair, shelves with books, a portable pottery fireplace we brought back from Mexico; the windows have bamboo shades we got on sale at Sears. We feel temporary and disoriented here, but by making the living room presentable, we try to maintain the illusion that despite having two children under three, we haven't given up on being

48

civilized. This is a recent development: In the smaller house we had before this one, we let everything go to hell, but now we've even bravely put an ashtray on the coffee table and set out knick-knacks on the higher bookshelves.

This has already created friction. With their homing devices tuned to whatever is valuable and therefore tabu, Keith and Nicole have been attracted to our favorite objects. I have screamed at them dozens of times about their not fiddling with them, I have slapped their little hands, growled in their little faces, removed them bodily from the room to find something else for them to be interested in. None of these are permanent solutions—which is the most exasperating thing about dealing with children: Something must be done over and over, like practicing a musical instrument, before any improvement is seen. Some children are like good dogs when it comes to learning, but mine seemed to be more like our cats, who had to be backhanded off the breakfast table three hundred times before they would even so much as flinch when you walked into the room and caught them up there again.

Mounted on the living room wall, about three feet over the sofa, stands a cabinet. This is no ordinary cabinet. It has a wooden frame with glass sides and glass doors. Set into the two hinged doors are stained-glass mosaics. When the light comes through the clear side panels, the doors are softly illuminated and show off the amber, red, yellow and green glass pieces skillfully and carefully fit to make a pleasing design. I'm proud of this cabinet. My father made it and gave it to me.

On the three glass shelves inside I have artfully arranged the pieces from a pottery chess set I purchased in Mexico. It has survived several moves and a car wreck. Unlike many of the garish and clumsy examples of Mexican folk art, the pieces of this set are finely crafted and painted, with subtle colors. In addition to these pieces, I have carefully placed the crowning glory of the display—a chess set made by my mother especially for me. The pieces are crafted from stained glass with lead bases, so that they are a pleasing combination of beauty and heft—they can be both admired and used.

Is this called asking for it? Is this like putting out your best china and silver for a genteel buffet then allowing a pack of bikers to attend your party? I should have seen it coming, but at the time I wanted to believe we had already passed though the stage when we could not have anything untouchable in the house (always projecting into the future, hoping, perhaps, that living in it would bring it sooner).

I have had plenty of warning. I have removed Keith from the tops of the tables and the cabinets and the bookshelves (a bookshelf was, to him, merely a ladder); I have tried to teach him that although household furniture bears a vague similarity to the playground equipment he is allowed to climb on outside, there is a very critical distinction to learn.

It is morning; I am upstairs writing, wresting a little order out of chaos. I hear a tremendous crash, the slapstick sound of a waiter with a full tray of dishes being tripped up when he comes strolling out of the kitchen.

I dash downstairs, my heart pounding, full of anxiety that someone has been hurt.

When I turn the corner into the living room, I see Keith standing on the couch, one foot still up on the back of it, frozen, wide-eyed, staring at me as if I am the tangible manifestation of his worst nightmare.

On the floor lies the cabinet. The glass doors are shattered. Scattered across the floor are a thousand shards of pottery and glass, headless queens and bishops, pawns smashed to smithereens. Instantly, the room is filled with flashing bone and blood-colored lights, like a disco strobe, flickering, blinding me. A white heat like a lightning bolt strikes me dumb, and even though I clench my fists and stand frozen in helplessness, inside I'm a missile blossoming upward out of its own fire. For a millisecond I'm at the epicenter of a bomb blast: This is the moment when Destruction that cares for nothing or no one is let loose in the world, when the promising teenage violinist is killed in a wreck caused by an elderly drunk who survives without a scratch, the moment when a burglar steals a trunk containing the widow's bundle of love letters written by her husband.

Trembling, I stand at the threshold. I can't enter the room. I can't touch Keith or even speak to him. I can do nothing but turn and walk slowly back upstairs, feeling as though my head is a weird jack-o'-lantern bobbing about the eaves outside the house, detached from my neck. I sit at my desk trying not to cry, telling myself over and over that objects are not important, that it's silly to care that much for something inanimate in the first place, that he's only an innocent, healthy child. I tell myself that it's a good thing he wasn't hurt, even if I can see in the darkness under my relief the wish that he would have been.

It's an even better thing that I didn't hurt him. I controlled my anger. But it's shocking to feel a rage so strong that it could make me kill my own child for a few chess pieces.

# THREE

## Snakes in the Yard

In early 1974 I won the Dobie-Pasiano Fellowship at the University of Texas, which provided a monthly stipend and residence at a ranch near Austin for a year in which to write.

Janice and I discussed the practical problems, chief of which was money. As always, we were poor. The stipend was not large enough to allow Janice to quit working, not that she wanted to. She had just gotten a good start on what was to be her career in television producing public affairs documentaries. If I were to take the fellowship, I would have to leave my family in Missouri. The only viable way I could do it would be essentially to live at the ranch and commute the 600 miles back home once a month for a few days.

I was set on taking the fellowship. As always, Janice was supportive of my life as a writer. She approved of my ambition and had faith in me; she was willing to raise two children without me while I was away. To help her, we

had the college-age daughter of friends live in the house
and serve as an au pair.

When I told people that I was going to Texas alone, I
sometimes received looks of curiosity, reproach or envy.
Now I realize that some may have wondered how this
would affect my marriage and my children. I didn't wonder—then. I was so hungry for recognition that I couldn't
bear to turn down the offer. Also, Janice and I had a tacit
understanding that we were "career people" who admired
each other's ambition. I took pride in supporting her career, wearing my raised consciousness like a badge. At the
time, I thought she was as ambitious as I was, but now I've
come to think that I was more ambitious for her than she
was for herself, that I needed for her to be ambitious so
that she wouldn't be emotionally dependent—that would
mean that we would have to be intimate, and that was
terrifying. I had urged her to get into television just as I
had picked out our graduate school, had moved us to Missouri, had talked her into going to Mexico and had brought
us to the farm—I had practiced the conventionally respectable bullying that males are allowed. So it went with
this decision to take the fellowship: We arranged our lives
according to my convenience.

We never said a word about whether my motives included the desire to escape, to be alone, about whether
we might drift apart because of the separation, whether
the children would suffer, whether it was unfair of me once
again to have determined our lives for purely selfish motives. Instead we talked about paying bills and scheduling
my visits.

When I struck out on the drive to Texas, I didn't know
what lay ahead, but that was half the point. I missed Keith
and Nicole immediately and felt guilty about leaving Janice
with the burden of child-raising. Yes, she had day-care and

the au pair, but she still had to work ten hours a day at her job only to come home to face an evening of chores before she could sleep. Feeling guilty was a small price to pay for the opportunity I had just seized, and it bought me temporary peace of mind. Going was a "wise career move" too, of course.

I didn't know then that I was rehearsing for when I would later leave for good.

The poet Jiménez said "you have in solitude only what you take there with you," and that ran through my mind during my first week at the ranch. I was alone for the first time in so long I could hardly recall it. The ranch—265 acres of limestone bluffs and richly fallow pastures cut by creeks and crumbling rock fences—lay only twenty minutes west of Austin, but when you came through the locked gate onto the property no other human could be seen or heard. Going to sleep at night, I would hear no other human sound but my own breathing and my pulse thumping in my ears. Outside, an armadillo rooting under the propane tank would knock its armored tail against the hollow metal cylinder with a clank, or deer, having crept into the yard, would be spooked suddenly and I'd hear a sneeze followed by a short burst of cloven hooves on the grass before they'd leap the fences. Owls, now and then a coyote, barking dogs. For a few nights I was awake listening to these night noises, apprehensive for my safety, apprehensive for my family far away in Missouri.

At first, being alone made me utterly self-conscious. I observed how my hands and arms moved in the air, heard my thoughts sound as loud as conversational speech, had the exasperating compulsion to announce to myself in present tense everything I did as I was doing it. *Now I am peeling carrots,* I would hear in my head as I was peeling carrots. Reaching the end of a writing spell, I would hike along the creeks or on top of the bluffs, hearing my own thrashing through the grass, keeping an eye out for rattlers, thinking about pioneers—and was suddenly aware that I had not had this strange feeling of playing by myself since my first five years of life, before my brother was born. My mother would push me out the back door into the yard and I would explore, alone, what seemed then to be the limitless boundaries of forest and shrubbery, with little sheds hidden in the woods, where I might stumble—it wouldn't have surprised me—upon the candy cottage where the witch in "Hansel and Gretel" lived, or the home of the Seven Dwarves.

Once I climbed along a narrow ledge about midway up the bluff over the creek. It was a path used by deer and goats; to follow it I had to do some cliff-face rock-climbing, and at one point I had to crawl under an overhang. I scooted along, seeing far below in the creek a copper-colored turtle probably the size of a dinner plate, but from here it was only a dirty penny in the green water. I thought of how, if I should fall, I might lie in the boulders and brush below for days with broken bones before anybody might discover me. *My poor children, fatherless!* A moment later, I turned my head and was nose to nose with a coiled-up rattler.

It had been drowsily sunning itself when I startled it. Its vibrating tail-tip sent off a ratcheting that a dozen cicadas could not have matched; my face was so close to its head I could see the vertical slits in its pupils. I was afraid to blink. I could not even move back quickly without fear of losing my grip on the ledge and plunging into the undergrowth below. My hands broke out in a sweat. I tried to ease myself back very gradually, thinking as I did of how in Boy Scouts they always told us to freeze when a rattler rattles and not make any abrupt movement that the snake might interpret as threatening. If it had struck me in the face there would be no place to put a tourniquet except around my neck; by the time I'd have climbed down from the bluff—slowly and carefully, to prevent the poison from spreading quickly through my system—and walked very calmly a mile up the dirt road to the gate and then another two miles or so to the highway, my head would be the size of a basketball and I would not likely be conscious.

Since I was prone on the ledge, I dragged myself backward by using my toes, and after a few moments, the edge of the rock protected me from the rattler. It continued to buzz for a bit, but then it unwound and slid away. I lay for several minutes completely drenched in sweat, my heart thundering, limbs trembling. The trapper, alone in the wilderness of the Rockies, has a close call with an angry rattler.

And wasn't it, well, thrilling? I knew I shouldn't have been crawling up there without letting someone know; I was being an irresponsible father, but the risk gave me an undeniable high. That I was completely alone magnified the pleasure.

Then there were moments of serenity, when my capacity for thought was lulled to sleep by the absence of another speaking human and my mind would empty of language. This was not vegetating, for my skull held a pleasant hum that made me attentive to my surroundings. One October afternoon I sat down by the creek on a flood-washed boulder scanning the bluffs on the other side of the water for whatever life was there. The sunlight was strong and not a breath of wind was stirring. All motion on the planet had ceased. I could hear no sound but that odd feedback in my own auditory canals. I was existing for a moment in an Eliot Porter photograph. Then a leaf from the very top of a sycamore broke loose. It took four days to reach the water. I studied it every inch of the way. There was no one to tell about this, no one I might feel compelled to point it out to, so I took it all in from start to finish without a lapse in concentration.

The flip side of this delicious solitude was loneliness and boredom. It might begin, this inversion, the way lake water upturns in August, putting the muck on the surface. Looking in the mirror, I'd wish I could see someone else's face. That would spread to a desire to think someone else's thoughts, have someone else's history, live someone else's life. In the kitchen cabinets I'd find only food that I, a very boring person, had bought. Reading, writing, playing the guitar became distasteful chores. I could listen to the radio, I told myself, except that I would only want to hear what *I* wanted to hear, and I was getting tired of that. So the only way I could enjoy listening to the radio would be to force myself to listen to something I didn't want to hear. I felt like a ten-year-old in the middle of summer vacation.

My grandiose aspirations were beginning to pall, and I longed to be happy doing something simple. I'd get *angst* and *ennui* and *weltschmerz* all at once, then I'd heap self-pity on top of them to make a great big sour banana split that turned my stomach. I'd pace about the empty house, cup my hands around my mouth and yell, "Halloooo out there! Anybody there?" Even pounding my pud was no more exciting than trimming my toenails.

I'd be struck with a longing for Janice and the kids. The longer I was at the ranch, the more I'd miss them. During the week before I was due to go home, I'd think about them constantly. I remembered Keith's sturdy little body, how he loved to ride on my back, how we used to feed a neighbor's pigs when we lived in the country, throwing them the slop, and during hot weather how he loved to spray the happy hogs with a garden hose to cool them. I remembered Nicole's pigtails, that very fine blonde hair, how she loved to ride on my shoes with her hands grabbing my belt. I remembered their spontaneous cuteness—"What do you want to be when you grow up, Keith?" His answer: "A policeman or a bird!"—and their clean smell. I had a snapshot of them in my wallet—the one I still have—standing together on a concrete stoop, at attention, grinning sheepishly and shyly, Nicole biting her lower lip, the two of them holding hands. They're wearing sneakers the size of little bathtub boats, and Nicole has on a kind of painter's smock, appropriate attire for a person holding up a sample of her art work.

I missed them terribly. It was during this period—my time away at the ranch—that I wrote the kids a story about a bull that kept running off to a neighbor's pasture only to miss his mama cow and the calves. All bleary-eyed and nostalgic, I'd shop for gifts to take back. Thinking ahead to the weekend (I usually arrived on Thursday night and stayed until Monday or Tuesday morning) would be a constant distraction. I would dream about holding the kids, reading to them, eating meals together, going to the park. Then I'd imagine being with Janice, making love, hugging and holding another person.

It was a twelve-hour drive from the ranch to the small house in Missouri to which they had moved just prior to my leaving, and invariably I would leave earlier than planned because I couldn't wait to hit the road. But the trip itself was grueling and anxiety-ridden. My vehicle was a worn-out VW bus with an inadequate heater, a puny engine, and the distressing habit of burning out its voltage regulators en route to anywhere important. In Oklahoma, the two-lane blacktop was occupied by 18-wheelers that planted their shiny wide bumpers in my rear-view mirror and twenty-year-old pickups driven by elderly Indians who used the center line like a foot path.

Red-eyed, back aching, I'd pull in after dark and go inside to greet Janice and the kids. They seemed happy enough to see me, but there was no ceremony, here. My reentries always made me vaguely frustrated and discontented; they would be going about the normal routine of their week night evenings, with baths and bedtime, and nothing would be suspended merely because I was arriving. Oh, hello there! How've you been? If you'll just pardon me for a moment . . . Janice's failure to make my homecoming extraordinary hurt me, although in fairness I admit I would have been asking her to add still another burden in a very busy day if I expected a special dinner or a tidy bedroom.

I wanted a ceremony that outwardly expressed what I felt—happy to be back—a ceremony that showed her feelings were likewise. Instead, I felt like a neighbor who stops by unexpectedly and gets caught between staying because the hostess has politely asked him to and leaving because he recognizes that this is a bad time to drop in.

I would pitch in to bathe the kids and read bedtime stories, all the while wedging my presents into the normal routine and wishing we could have a party. Then, kids in bed, I'd begin my descent into wretchedness—trying to coax an aloof, harried woman with a migraine into enjoying her conjugal duties. Thinking ahead to this night while driving, I would already have hardened and melted a dozen times until my lust had gone, like hunger, beyond the sharpness of urgent need and into some odd nausea.

Wanting her so much made me fear she would reject me—not put me off, exactly, but not *want* me, either—making me a panting, undignified supplicant. I'd be allowed to do what I needed. But then I'd complain about how she wasn't *interested* in me any more, I'd grow angry at myself for groveling then angry at her for making me crawl. For God's sake, why didn't she long to have me here the way I longed to be here?

Carrying these bruises into Saturday, I'd feel mistrust set in. Old specters of betrayal. "Are you having lovers?" "Don't be absurd. When would I have time?" She refused to reassure me; instead, she defended her virtue on the very slender grounds of opportunity. Why couldn't she grab me and grin and say, "I never want another man but you!" whether she meant it or not, and then show me her desire as proof?

She was probably angry with me for being gone. But, true to her nature and to our relationship, she couldn't express this directly and instead found a way to punish me. What she said was that I couldn't expect to pop in once a month and have the regular routine of their lives completely suspended or rearranged. I couldn't be gone weeks then expect her to jump immediately into bed as if I had been here all along.

That was entirely reasonable. Or it would have sounded so to a reasonable person, an outside observer perhaps, but I was not one. I was carrying the baggage of our difficult interpersonal history with me. Not too many months before this she had declared, without inviting me to discuss it, that she was going to have a tubal ligation, so that she could get off the Pill. A vasectomy for me would have been less complicated, less dangerous and less expensive, so I asked her why she'd made this choice. "Because I'm the one who would get pregnant," she said. She was allowing for the possibility of getting pregnant even if I had a vasectomy. I was hurt because she didn't think it was necessary to discuss this and because the arrangement had a dark, implied premise that gnawed at my security. She went ahead and had the operation, and I kept my mouth shut about my misgivings and my wounded pride.

Was I being unfair? Did I expect too much? Or should I have been so grateful for my opportunity that I should have been content to think of my homecoming as a mere changing of the guard, as if I were a friend who dropped by to help? And what was her life like, there without me? She wasn't talking; she seemed to be holding her breath, drumming her fingers on the table, as it were, waiting for me to get out of her hair.

Twice in a row these reunions wound up with my driving back in a sulk, melancholy that nothing had been renewed, depressed to be stuck in a twilight zone where my life was not truly whole in either location. I considered this estrangement to be an unforeseen and unfortunate side effect of my decision and hoped it was only temporary; I tried to pass it out of my mind. Avoiding a direct confrontation with my problems was an old habit; if forced to recognize that a problem was looming up on the left, say, I liked to stand in the road and mark time, hoping it would cross in front of me and be gone by the time I reached the intersection.

*Meanwhile, back at the ranch . . .* I took my editor, fresh from New York, on a walking tour. I pointed out several large and very live diamond-back rattlers living in the nooks and crannies of the old stone walls and under an ancient cabin off in an isolated corner of the property. On the creek I pointed out some cottonmouth moccasins, telling him how much more venomous they were than rattlesnakes and how much less willing they were to share territory with humans, how they sometimes came after you in the water where you were swimming. I told him the old legend about the guy who went water-skiing and fell off

62

into a nest of moccasins all knotted up in a big ball. (I told him it happened to a friend of a friend just to make the story better.) I told him I had seen copperheads here, too, and how someone reported to have spotted a coral snake—small, timid nocturnal creatures whose venom will kill in a matter of minutes—one night in the front yard. Oh, there was snake lore galore! His eyes grew wide, this tenderfoot, and he kept moving his feet about even when we were sitting indoors. I chuckled. I poo-pooed his twitching. Flaunting my machismo, I told him about my encounter with the rattler on the bluff. I was used to living with danger, I said.

Now I know I was warming up to something.

The things that do me no credit are the hardest to tell. Through my publisher I got a letter from a woman praising my first novel. She lived in a nearby city, and she reminded me that we had known one another in high school, which was unnecessary: My mind was suddenly awash with over-heated memories of us at age sixteen in the back seat of my parents' car out on a country road, heaving, slobbering and panting, doing what was then called heavy petting and never going "all the way."

She was now a grown woman, married, with two children, educated, responsible, articulate and perhaps not even aware as I was that something had been put on hold. Did she feel as I did that we had had eighteen years of foreplay? Her letter was friendly but not personal.

I invited her and her family to the ranch. I kept telling myself that if we got together it only would be like former classmates meeting to catch up on news and to satisfy that especially piquant curiosity we have about people we have not heard about in years. But by the time the visit was over, she and I had tacitly agreed to meet again without her spouse and children. Before that happened, I tortured

63

myself with the probability of what I was about to do. Aside from a kiss or two that lingered beyond respectability under the mistletoe at a drunken office party, I had been a faithful husband. Now, though, I wondered whether my good behavior had less to do with my sterling character than with cowardice.

I concentrated on making things palatable to my conscience. I thought schmuck thoughts. Oily, slippery thoughts that slid right past the censors on greased rails. First, there was getting even: Janice owed me at least one. Then, there was the cosmic outlook, how insignificant, a thousand years from now, a little adultery would look in the greater scheme of things. When you matched it up against the eternal clockwork of the stars, this tiny motion was no more visible than a quark. All around the planet on both its light and dark sides, at any moment some man and woman were having a bit of the slap and tickle at the expense of their spouses. I knew several men who thought nothing about one-night stands, and I knew at least one husband who was aware that his wife had a lover and shrugged it off. I knew one very perfectly respectable professional chap who had knowingly married a lesbian and allowed his wife to bring her female lovers home to stay. Beside this kind of kinky hanky-panky an old-fashioned, low-rent rendezvous looked prosaic, conventional. Here these pioneers were striking out in daring exploration, and I was still struggling with a decision to take a first timid step. That I would even worry about it made me seem hopelessly stodgy.

Writers were famous for philandering. The bios of the Nobel laureates showed how their passion and love of "beauty" simply spilled over, couldn't be contained by the flimsy mores of middle-class society. Obviously, then, I owed it to my career to hump my old girlfriend.

I was half hoping our groping would be a tawdry, disappointing one-nighter that satisfied my curiosity and earned me whatever merit badge I was working for. This wasn't the case. Horror of horrors—it was loads of furtive fun, and I was tormented by the desire to repeat it. In all the fancy, nimble-footed brainwork that had brought me here, I hadn't reckoned on a messy, complicated *affair*.

Nor had I imagined I'd feel guilty. I was learning the difference between being betrayed and betraying. Being the victim had been far more comfortable, it dumped everything outward, gave me an object to focus all my anger on and oddly increased my sense of worth: I could tell myself I had been far too good to be treated that way. Now, being the betrayer, everything boomeranged. It made me sick of myself. I couldn't even have the pleasure of looking into the mirror, winking, and saying "You rascal, you!" because I knew now how I had tricked myself into doing this. I couldn't trust myself any more.

Since I had already stepped across the line, though, I could not get any *more* guilty, could I? The wretchedness I felt wouldn't likely increase in direct proportion to the number of transgressions (in fact, the opposite's true), so I went for seconds and thirds. Now, however, I refused to pretend this was anything but hoggish rutting. I saw winks from the motel desk clerk, and once—an all-time low—we used the back seat of her car parked in a cold garage while her children were asleep and her husband was away.

She asked me whether she should divorce her husband. That shook me awake. It was one thing to be a philandering rascal and quite another to be a homewrecker, and I was suddenly frightened to think that I was risking my own marriage as well. I advised her to confess to her husband

and go to a marriage counselor. She didn't know if telling him was such a good idea, but she knew from my advice that my part in this was over.

I was never good at keeping secrets. The bigger the secret, the stronger my urge to tell. Now that I had reformed, my guilt festered like an inflamed wound, so on my next trip back to Missouri, I confessed.

"Oh, for God's sake!" Janice declared, furious. "Why'd you have to tell me that? Sure, you've got a bad conscience and you just had to get this off your chest, and now you feel better, but you just made *me* feel bad! That's not fair!"

I certainly had gotten her attention by coming clean. She fumed for a day or so but calmed down more quickly than I had presumed she would. At first I was relieved, but then her reaction kept replaying in my inner ear, producing suspicion. Her philosophy was that hidden things should be kept covered, that what you do not know does not hurt you. I hadn't known that about her.

I had expected my confession to make everything clear and open between us. As the guilty party, I felt I had no right to be suspicious and I knew that guilt itself could cause suspicion. But I couldn't help but speculate on what else there might be that I did not know about her. And then I learned that wondering about what you do not know can, indeed, hurt you.

# FOUR

## Bosom of the Family

We agreed healing was called for. So Janice quit her job in early spring and brought the kids and dogs and cats to join me at the ranch for the remainder of my fellowship. The season was right for regenerating. Fields surrounding the house were thick with Indian paintbrush, gaillardias, coreopsis, wine cups, bluebonnets and cornflowers, and on the rocky ridges the prickly pear sported blossoms behind their ears. Wild plums were flowering along the creek, and the pear tree beside the back shed showered the ground with its spent blossoms after a rain.

Mornings I wrote in the shed attached to the old barn behind the house. Then, after lunch, Janice and I took the kids down to the creek, where, dressed in swim suits and old sneakers, we'd wade or let them practice swimming in the deeper places where the water was so clear you could drop a penny in and see it weave and bob as it descended twelve feet to settle on the limestone bottom. We took inner tubes upstream to the western boundary of the property and floated lazily down to where the water broadened into rocky shallows. I made the kids bows and arrows out of willow limbs, and we hiked up to the tops of the bluffs and shot the arrows into space over the creek. Nights, we would creep up on armadillos while they rooted for grubs in the yard—they don't hear well—then we'd tap on their shells as if knocking on a door and holler, and they'd hop straight in the air for about a foot. When they alighted, they'd run around us in circles while we screamed with laughter.

Both sets of grandparents were only an hour away, and sometimes we'd ship the kids off for a visit so that Janice and I could go to the creek alone, where we'd skinny-dip and lie nude on sun-baked boulders, turning ourselves as if on spits and lazily making love like the world's first couple in Eden. When we felt the need, we invited friends to stay and spent enormously pleasant evenings dining and drinking in candlelight on the porch, listening to the low, sibilant rush of the water over stones down at the creek. Without television, we had time to talk or dawdle in the roomy kitchen and test recipes for our mammoth zucchini crop; there was space in our lives for taking trips as a family, and we spent several days at the beach in Corpus that summer.

My second novel was published during the summer, was reviewed widely and well and was sold to a paperback house for reprinting; it was also optioned for a movie, and I was hired to write an adaptation, bringing me more income as a writer than I had ever had before. So it seemed to me that my personal and professional lives were aligning like benign moons in some fortuitous arrangement that boded well for the future.

But neither of us had definite future plans. We longed to stretch this present life or approximate it somewhere, perhaps by moving to Austin, but the overcrowded job market made it impossible. Just before my fellowship ended, I went to Los Angeles to work on the adaptation, and the children went to stay with their grandparents; Janice interviewed at a network affiliate in a large Rust Belt city and was offered a job as an anchorwoman and reporter.

I welcomed learning new street names, new history, new mores, modes of dress and speech and thought. Since I couldn't duplicate in any way the serene, pastoral pleasures of the ranch, it seemed a good idea to fling myself into a radically different experience. I had sufficient income as a writer for the moment that I wouldn't have to look for official employment, and Janice's salary represented a 300 percent increase in her previous pay.


In the Rust Belt City we lived in a rambling brick house with a huge dry basement—that was a first for us—a fireplace, wall-to-wall carpeting, a modern kitchen and a garden room I converted to a study. It was set on a huge, tree-shaded corner lot in a staunchly middle-class neighborhood. Up and down the street were kids on bikes and Big Wheels, and our next-door neighbor was the librarian at the elementary school our children would later attend. It made me feel like a solid citizen. Living here, I couldn't continue to think of myself as a hippie; we had emerged into a new phase of adult life.

Out of guilt and a sense of fair play, I jumped into playing househusband. I rose before anyone else, cooked up pots of oatmeal festooned with raisins and sometimes coconut, dressed the kids while Janice was readying for work and drove them to a kindergarten and day-care center not far away. Mornings I wrote in my redone garden room. I spent my afternoons shopping and running the errands that are the bane of any suburban hausfrau's existence—

to the cleaners, to the library, to the hardware store, to the gas station, to the grocery, to the bank.

Those afternoons I learned the rut of shopping mall parking lots, of opening, shutting, locking and unlocking the car door a hundred times an afternoon, struggling to make the rounds before the hubby gets home, fuming in gridlock traffic knowing that if you don't reach the day-care center before they lock their doors your children will be cast out to play in the street. Feeling my life dribble away as I crossed out items on my daily list, I began to wonder how these trivial *things* ever came to be so infuriatingly necessary.

Being home alone, I felt a weird loneliness set in. Standing in line at a supermarket check-out, I came to understand why I had to wait for what seemed a decade while an elderly widow chatted with the checker, came to understand precisely why some old man would never reach for his checkbook until his groceries had already been totaled: It had nothing to do with being inconsiderate of those in line behind him; it was done purely from a need to stall for time to say another sentence or two to the friendly young checker, about the weather, about crabgrass or coffee, wanting to trade human noises like so many small consoling strokes. The supermarket is a clean, well-lighted place.

After shopping, I'd prepare dinner. I was learning to cook. It was nonverbal fun, and the results were edible—something I can't say for failed manuscripts—if not always pleasing. I stuck to recipes that could be produced in a half hour, kid-meals such as Kraft macaroni and cheese mixed with tuna. I went from there to pot roasts and fried chicken. At first vegetables went from a can to a saucepan to the table, then I learned to steam fresh ones. I learned to my astonishment that staples I had presumed were

70

easy to prepare because they were so common—one-word foods such as "rice" and "gravy"—took a finesse that comes only from training.

For a time, I got interested in fancy Jell-O salads, bought animal-shaped molds, made lime-green stuff with cottage cheese and nuts, orange stuff with carrots and raisins, cherry stuff with fruit cocktail. Your basic Methodist potluck supper gelatin concoctions sitting on a limp lettuce leaf.

After the newness of it wore off, cooking became a dreary chore. My imagination went limp when I tried to conceive of something other than my basic four meals, those being the culinary equivalent of the lowest common denominator—they were what was left after everyone's objections had whittled down my repertoire. Now and then I interjected a thrill, a homespun variation on the tried and true: Once I made macaroni and cheese from scratch, but everyone had already become hopelessly addicted to the quick-fix kind, and mine was not "orange" enough.

I took pride in being confident enough in my masculinity that doing what wives traditionally did would not harm my ego. Occasionally, wearing an apron made me feel like a cross-dresser and I did have moments of uneasiness. Then, too, Janice had become a local celebrity, and I was learning what it felt like to be identified as the less important spouse. Though this was not humiliating, it was humbling. It was hard for anybody to take me seriously as a "real" writer because no "real" writer would tolerate living in a dull, Midwestern city. Some "real" writers had spent formative years in such places but had gone elsewhere to achieve fame and fortune.

We, too, were only marking time, waiting to go. In the meantime a few milestones were quietly passed.

One summer night Keith and Nicole decided that they

and a friend would sleep in the backyard. The idea made me anxious; I had visions of abductors catching the whiff of unprotected babies riding on the breeze—the yard had only a rail fence around it, and one long side of the back was exposed to a street. Janice calmed me down, however, as usual. I decided to let them do it. I remembered the first time I'd ever slept outside the house, how curious I had been about what happened out there after I went to sleep inside.

The kids had a pup tent, and they and a boy from up the street took blankets, a portable radio, a flashlight, a little bow and arrow and provisions (cookies, raisins, popcorn) for the long siege of darkness to come. Until we went to bed around ten, they kept traipsing in and out of the house to retrieve items they wanted for this journey through the night—a stuffed animal, a doll, an extra pillow, a candle—"No, you can't have any candles out there!"

Then came taps. We turned the lights off in the house. For a few minutes I thought I might sleep, but I soon realized I was far too excited. I went into their dark bedroom and looked out the window into the backyard. I could see the flank of the pup tent in the darkness. The beam of the flashlight danced on the canvas. I heard Nicole whine, "Let me hold it, Keith!" and Keith reply, "No, it's still my turn!" I could picture them lying on their blankets inside the closed-up tent, cozy, their hearts beating, eyes open wide, alert to the possibilities of the unknown.

I couldn't resist making a sneak attack as the Bogey Man; it seemed obligatory, traditional, as if I were compelled to play under cover of night the role assigned to me in a child's nightmare, every dad's dark side, acting out our worst mutual fears for their safety and exorcising the demon by giving him a form.

Gleefully, I slipped out the front door and made my

way into the librarian's side yard, where I slid along the rail fence until I was close to the back of the pup tent. I hunkered in the darkness. Keith said he was hot and wanted to open the tent flaps, but Nicole objected. "Things'll get in," she said. Bugs, maybe. Something *out there* might come inside. "Jimmy, quit getting cookies all crumbled up all over my blankets!" Keith complained.

Then they began trying to scare each other, Keith telling how he knew this kid who had gone camping and a bear had come and ripped a hole in the tent and had eaten a kid's leg off. "You think a bear could do that to this tent?" Nicole asked. Keith laughed like Dracula.

Squatting in the darkness, surrounded by the night, I eavesdropped with a sense of peculiar loss and wonder. It seemed amazing that these little humans I had spawned had reached an age at which they were able to converse without my aid or presence. They had become autonomous, capable of existing without my supervision; the momentum of their lives had reached some critical mass so that even were I to go back inside, they might continue to talk or sleep or eat or laugh or argue, and I would have no inkling of the myriad complexities that would form the content of this experience for them. Their lives had become their own.

But before I gave them over to the night, I had a duty to remind them that danger lay ahead, that they still needed me. I made a soft low growl and rattled some leaves. Instantaneous silence in the tent.

"What was that sound?" Nicole whispered urgently.

"Oh, it's probably just Daddy," Keith said more loudly than he would have had he truly believed this.

I emitted a wart-hog grunt.

"Daddy?" Nicole called out fearfully.

"All right, Daddy, we know it's you!" Keith challenged.

"What if it's not?" Nicole hissed.

I scratched on the tent with a stick. All three screamed then Keith yelled, "Okay, you can stop now!" I suddenly shot my arm under the side of the tent and howled like a werewolf. They grabbed my arm and pounded on it with their fists with a ferocity born of fear, until I hollered in a pitiful voice to be released. I let them vanquish the beast.

A month later, and only minutes after they were born it seemed, there came a September morning when we tucked boxes of crayons, blunt-tipped scissors and Big Chief writing tablets under their arms and sent them off to first grade: the first day of a very long journey guaranteed to be full of marvelous and terrible adventures. I envied them. I remembered the smell and taste of library paste and how it dried and felt crumbly like sleep-crust in your eyes, or boogers. I remembered learning to read a clock; how the nuns in parochial school told us to pray before we went home for lunch because we might get struck down by a truck. And always Dick and Jane and Spot and Puff ran, ran, ran. I remembered how I'd learned to insert "under God" into the Pledge of Allegiance I had already memorized, how I had to stand in a corner for breaking my milk bottle, how I'd had a gold star pasted to my forehead after winning a spelling bee.

We got them up much too early. Janice took their picture in front of the fireplace after they were ready for school. The snapshot shows two happy tow-heads, a handsome set of twins, their cheeks pressed together, holding hands. If they had apprehension they hid it well. Keith has on a navy long-sleeved t-shirt with a large bird appliqued on the breast, and his new jeans, not yet washed, are a little long, so the material bunches up on his thighs; Nicole is wearing a knee-length denim smock with a patchwork ruffle hem and a large white collar. Her long blonde hair has been braided and the silky ropes are pinned with ribbons to the top of her head. Her hair was so fine that I'd have to wash it with a "tangle-free" shampoo and spend a long time afterward trying to brush out the snags while she would fret and flinch and whine.

Sending them off into this wondrous maze of astonishing pleasures and punishments was an occasion of great moment. I knew they would do well; they had sat in our laps and heard all of the Dr. Seuss books so many times that they could open, say, *The Cat in the Hat* themselves and turn the pages while they recited the story, recognizing some of the words, filling in the rest from memory; they could count, they knew the alphabet, and their kindergarten teachers had always praised their alertness and curiosity. Rhodes scholars, I thought. Ivy League grad schools. Better start saving.

Then came the first snowstorm they would later be able to recall clearly. One week in January the Canadian jet stream slammed a blizzard down across a huge swatch of Midwestern prairie, dumping several feet of snow, and in the aftermath, the interstates north from our city to Chicago and east to Columbus and Pittsburgh were frozen shut. The news showed footage shot from choppers of derelict semis strewn at crazy angles like dozens of partially opened jackknives spilled onto the roads. Travelers stayed with their cars and were dug out and rescued if they didn't freeze to death first or asphyxiate themselves with their exhaust; some left their vehicles to seek aid, were lost in the swirling white fog and died of exposure. The papers would reveal how many homeless bums huddled in the corners of vacant buildings succumbed to the cold.

When the storm passed on to the east, the sun shone like a pearl button against a pale blue sky, but all across the city a dazzling blanket of white obscured all curbs and even fences, and nobody could move. The street in front of our house, normally a very busy artery for rush-hour traffic, was a field of snow, more vacant and quiet than even on a Christmas morning.

I stood at the bay window in long johns and wool socks with a mug of steaming coffee and watched, like an idle aquarium gazer, the smoke from my neighbor's fireplace rise in lazy coils into air so still the smoke simply dissolved in a solvent of sky. Perched about the parapets of his chimney, a crowd of sparrows jittered and bathed themselves in the rising heat. The outstretched arms of our walnut trees were bearing the weight of thick cables of snow laid along their biceps and forearms. Beside our front door was a tall evergreen (I never did learn my Yankee botany; the kids just called it "the Christmas tree"), and it sagged under the weight of snow on its shoulders; now and then a patch would disintegrate and crash onto the shoulder below, making the branch it vacated spring up and shake the next branch, and the tree would shudder and fling off a momentarily sunlit halo of snow dust, like a dog shaking off water.

I relished this. I loved the astounding quiet out there. A native Sun Belter, I learned how snow defines itself. It takes violent acts of nature to pull the plug on the ever-churning engine of the social order, but most of them—flood, fire, tornado—are cruelly disruptive, driving us out of our homes or destroying them. Snow, though, tucks us back into our caves to hibernate. It reminds us much more gently and benignly than flood or fire that nature is our master after all. It's as nice to look at as the ocean, and it sound-proofs all those raucous surfaces so that the silence conjures up serenity.

Curious about the rest of the city, we turned on the radio to hear a disk jockey chat with his engineer about how he had to walk to work this morning in waist-high drifts, "but not to school," he joked, then moved into his very long list of what would be closed today, though it was obvious from looking out the window that nature had forced a moratorium on all banking, baking, and maybe even bur-gling. There'd be no selling or installing, putting up or tearing down, not even any novel writing. We could all sit on our duffs all day without having to worry about some-body else out there getting ahead. Whatever we planned to do out there, we wouldn't get to do it, and it wasn't our fault. Funny how it didn't matter so much now, even looked a little trivial in contrast to the more forceful stamp, a mere swipe of hand, it seems, nature put on things outside. You will surrender, or else.

As I say, I didn't need the radio to tell me what was closed. Still, it was nice to hear the list read. The drone assured me that this was happening to everyone else, too; it told me that my family was not alone with this, something I needed to know, for running just beneath the beauty like a soft but discordant pedal tone you barely notice was the reminder that here was danger, too. People get out there and catch their death.

Not much left to do, then, but enjoy it.

A neighbor called to say he was coming down the street with a large sled pulled by his St. Bernard. It was a winter tradition with him. Kids, ahoy! We dressed Keith and Ni-cole in layers—socks and galoshes, corduroys and t-shirts, sweat shirts over flannel shirts, coats and woolen caps, scarves and mittens that would be soaked within minutes. I bundled up to greet the arrival of the sled, which already had two tiny passengers clad in snowsuits, one yellow, one blue. Their hoods were drawn tight, leaving only their pink cameo faces free. The dog that pulled the rig was so tall he could look me in the eye if it weren't for his bangs, and when my kids sat down on the sled in front of the tots, the dog's wedge-shaped tail fanned their heads when he wagged it. My neighbor lead the dog along with a leash, and I watched them all glide down the center of the street with envy. I wished I had been small enough to get on board. I'd never been pulled in a sled by a dog.

Later, we tried to make a snowman and to toss snowballs, but the snow was still too dry and powdery. We made snow ice cream instead, getting big bowls of pristine snow and pouring a little vanilla and cream on it. We traipsed in and out of the house all afternoon, going out to play then coming in when the cold had made our wet hands and the tips of our ears brittle and sensitive. We left wet galoshes in the foyer and littered the floor with disks of compressed snow and leaves that melted and made a muddy mess, not that anyone—including me—cared.

Next morning, the schools were still closed. We could hear the snow plows scraping through the slush on the thoroughfare out front. Some people had had enough and for whatever reason wanted to crank up the status quo again, maybe get the jump on somebody else. Janice had to work. The noon news had to go on. The postal service had to treat their motto as a rule rather than the day as a rare exception. The convenience stores would have to live up to their names.

Keith, Nicole and I went out again. We had the second-day syndrome—we were looking for yesterday's fun. We'd gotten the dressing business down to a routine; knew which things tended to come untied and what leaks where.

One break turned out to be that the snow was quite ripe now, ready to be molded into whatever we wanted. We set out to make a snowman; at first the twins were babbling with plans to form the biggest and the best on the block. *Hey, we'll get one of Daddy's old coats and hats and scarves!*

But before long we settled for two rounded boulders of snow, one atop the other, with a third looking like a deflated basketball as the head. Before we were through, some boys came by to coax Keith into a tribal snowball fight and, while the missiles sailed overhead, Nicole and I decorated our poor stillborn monster by shoving a stick into the head for a nose before retreating.

The front yard became a battleground; some boys hastily scraped up a parapet of snow to duck behind while another band roamed throughout the yard, darting from tree to tree to lay siege. Then somebody said, "Hey, let's build a fort!" A truce was called while cardboard boxes were rounded up to use for molds—my idea, clever me—and within a few minutes they'd made several blocks and stacked them up for a wall. Then some other kids came by, a new fight started up, but then died. Somebody suggested going to Jimmy's yard because nobody'd touched the snow there. They ran off, giving war whoops. Nicole stayed behind. She was tired of being pelted.

She picked up a box. "Let's build a house," she said.

"Okay. An Eskimo house. An igloo."

While we formed the bricks, we told each other what we knew about Eskimos. What she knew was this: They wear furs from head to toe, have to crawl through a tunnel to get inside their houses and eat whales. I couldn't add much more—there's fishing for seals from kayaks, kissing by rubbing noses . . .

"Really?"

"Yeah." I was surprised she hadn't heard this.

"Why?"

Why, indeed? "I don't know. Sometimes they have more than one wife, too," I added impulsively, thinking immediately that this wasn't what I meant. I was thinking of Arab pashas, not Eskimos. "I mean that if an Eskimo likes you he will invite you to sleep with his wife." I suddenly realized that was over her head and I'd just as soon keep it that way. And was it even true?

"Huh," she says with a puzzled giggle. Obviously she took "sleep" at face value and couldn't quite see how doing this would be a gesture of friendship. But she also knew something naughty was going on.

We worked for a while until we completed two side walls and a back wall that came up to just about her eyes, but I knew the front tunnel was going to take more engineering and energy than I had. The unfinished snowman stood beside the instant parapet that became a wall that evolved into a half-finished fort that was no longer about to become an igloo. All my life, I'd trained myself to finish what I started; these half-formed structures were faintly disturbing. I chastised myself for not surrendering to the ceaselessly moving stream of childish play.

Nicole kept taking off one mitten and sticking her fingers in her mouth.

"What about a roof?" she asked.

"Aren't you cold?"

"Kinda."

Out on the street traffic was moving slowly but steadily. The plows had tossed up furrows of ice-encrusted slush on both sides of the street, and the car wheels sprayed these ridges with dirty slush. The tree trunks were wet and their limbs dripped ice water down the backs of our necks. Some soup would be nice, I remember thinking. Maybe hot coffee. The pleasure of taking off our boots and damp socks and drying our feet over the furnace grate.

The white blanket on the yard was now rent and tattered with scuff marks, boot prints, dog tracks. Here and there ugly patches of brown showed through. The walls of our intended igloo showed shredded leaves and sticks like some weird adobe, and it spoiled my idea of what igloo walls would look like. A thin overcast had turned the warm sunlight into a Polaroid haze.

"Why don't we go inside?"

"Okay. Just a minute."

Her voice had an odd echo. She was crouched down inside the walls and was giving them a peculiar scrutiny. She reached out and stroked one with a bare red hand, her brow furrowed in preoccupation. I think she may have been thinking of those Eskimos, how it would be to have ice-cold walls in a house you could not stand up in, how if your Eskimo daddy liked somebody he would let them sleep with your Eskimo mommy. I think she may have been trying to conjure up all that she might possibly know about icy houses and those who live inside them.

# FIVE

## "This Way to the Egress"

In 1979, Janice anchored weekends at a TV station. I baby-sat and worked on the house we had bought in a blue-collar neighborhood. During the week, I was a feature writer for a newspaper in the southwestern city we moved to after leaving Indiana. The cars, the yard and the house were my responsibilities expressly, but many of the house-keeping chores were mine, too. When I received no card from Janice on Father's Day, I began making plans to leave and was out of the house two months later.

Later, when I told Janice that this had been a turning point, she said, "People do the things that they feel they need to do; they shouldn't need any special thanks." She implied that I should be more mature than to expect re-wards for doing my duty. I had chosen to do these things; since she hadn't *asked* me to do them, she owed me no thanks.

But I also heard *I don't need you* in her remark. This was the voice of the self-sufficient German in her lineage. Once we had gotten out of a cab at an airport, and when I looked up after grabbing our bags, she was striding swiftly toward the terminal with a peculiar urgency, head down, hands before her, and after trotting to catch up, I found that she had slammed the cab door on her thumb, breaking the bone, and was looking for a first aid station. Her self-containment always made me feel superfluous.

Only a few months before this Father's Day, I had complained that I didn't feel close to her.

She said, "Promise me you won't leave me for another six months."

"Okay," I agreed, astonished.

This was the umpteenth occasion when we should have talked, but we dropped the subject. I hadn't wanted to leave her then, and I was complaining in the hopes that we could work on the problem. Her answer perplexed me. She had seemed unhappy for some time; why, I didn't know. Apparently I couldn't make her happy, and her answer suggested that she had figured out a way to get happy but the plan took six months to effect.

I don't pretend to understand her even now. After eighteen years of marriage, her essential nature was still a mystery to me. I could say that her favorite movie was *The Wizard of Oz,* that she envied and appreciated my ability to play like a kid with the kids, that she was fond of swimming and sailing and dancing, that she was conscientious in her job, that she loved the theater, that she was generous to strangers down on their luck, that she had enormous stores of perserverance and energy, that she was polite but aloof in social situations, that her speech was sometimes affected ("ad-VER-tiss-ment"), that she always hated her hair but was vain about her size (103 pounds; she would call herself "fat" at 106), that she was fond of driving, that she was sentimental about animals and plants (she had at one time wanted to be a veterinarian), that she had a predisposition to migraines and backaches and that she rarely told me what she really felt.

For all I did know about Janice, there was still so much I didn't know. What did she really want from the future? What did she really feel about me? What role did I really play in her life? Was she truly ambitious or had I merely insisted that she should be? How did she feel about my love-making? Did she really want our children? Why was she unhappy? What would make her happy?

Not only did I not know her, I felt unknown to her. I had complained that I wasn't close to Janice because I felt lonely. That people could be lonely in marriage was new and disturbing to me. When I was jogging, I'd pass a pair of lovers lying nose-to-nose in the grass and I'd feel a surge of almost uncontainable jealousy. I yearned to be in love.

What had kept me from feeling lonely before this was work. For a dozen years I had been writing seriously. For the first four of those years I had worked patiently and without recognition, and the results had been the publication of two novels in quick succession, a portfolio of respectable reviews, a couple of prizes, two grants, two paperback sales and a movie option. All that had occurred in two years' time. I applied the phrase "meteroric rise" to my career and presumed success was certain.

Then came a long dry spell in which I had to get a job. Meanwhile, my novels went out of print. The movie prospect dissipated. My rise was not meteoric, after all. As I fretted about it, I squirmed under the conditions of my nine-to-five job—every writer's nightmare—even though being a film critic and feature writer was worthwhile and interesting employment.

I was having a mid-life crisis so classic that I could have been stood like a cardboard cutout beside a sociologist's lecturn as a prop to illustrate a textbook discussion of it.

None of this I saw with any clarity. A fever had settled in my brain. My jaws ached from grinding my teeth in my sleep; I drank more, stayed out nights after screenings, looking for diversion. I felt bored, restless. I wished I'd had enough of the true bohemian spirit that I could hit the road for a while, let my wife take care of things, come back like some ramblin' gamblin' amblin' kind of guy with my guitar on my back and a bunch of new ballads about my adventures down in Mexico to sing to my kiddos. That I plodded to work day after day sober and dutiful made me feel like a drone.

*I want more,* I kept saying. More money, time off, recognition. I wanted to eat out more; I wanted to spend afternoons at a round table, bending elbows with my fellow writers; I wanted more interesting conversation, more interesting friends; I wanted, literally, a lot more living space— our house had no study, and I wrote in the dining room with my back to the foot traffic.

I wanted more flesh. All women became astonishingly attractive, and I flirted outrageously. The after-whiff of perfume that a passing woman would leave in her trail would almost reduce me to tears. In this strange state of hyperarousal I fixated hungrily on an essential quality of femininity as it was revealed in, say, the inward crook of an elbow, a curve of cheek, the delicacy of an ear lobe, the way their belts and buttons fastened the other way. I absorbed the rhythms and content of their speech—they were so much more interesting to listen to than were men, capable of so much more emotional nuance, subtle attitudinal posturing. And the content of their remarks was a heaping smorgasbord compared to which the men's steamtable buffet ran a pitiful second.

The sensations women aroused—an ill-defined mixture of lust and a broad, vague sensuality—were a constant in my life now. The external world had become supercharged and permeated with libidinous electricity. Everywhere about me things stood sharply outlined in their own fecund vibrancy and called to my blood, *This way to adventure!* Or maybe it was really more on the order of Barnum's old gag sign, THIS WAY TO THE EGRESS.

A quality of pubescent arousal lay in all this, the way I had felt when I was eleven or twelve and sat at my school desk and stared at the nape of Buena Lee Turner's neck; I felt such stirrings of protectiveness and curiosity and tenderness that I'd goose-pimple instantly, restraining my compulsion to stroke the fine strands that had evaded her mother's fingers when she had braided her daughter's hair into silky pigtails.

I started jogging longer, harder, faster, until I was up to ten-mile stretches on weekends. I was, I think, pursuing the adult equivalent of the advice my old Boy Scout manual gave to boys who felt "restless"—cold showers, sleeping with your hands outside the covers and getting right up in the mornings when you awake.

Apparently I wasn't running hard or fast enough. I had two brief affairs. When I confessed to Janice about them, I struggled to explain how these sensations seemed like a compulsion or a chemical addiction. "It's like I have some kind of weird flu," I said.

She snorted, shook her head. "You're just trying to say you're not responsible for your own actions," she declared.

I was guilty as charged. She equated me with the kind of schmuck who combed his hair over his bald spot, unbuttoned his shirt to his navel to show his gold chains and hung out at singles bars looking for some action. In my worst moments, I imagined that was who I had become, too, but in retrospect I see that I really wasn't promiscuous—I had no one-night stands. Inasmuch as I did go out looking for "action," I went no farther than it took to find someone who was eager to know all of me and to whom I could show myself.

The night I confessed, I didn't say ". . . and I'm moving out" or ". . . and I'm going to stop this." I was confused, and I was taking the coward's way out of letting Janice deal with my problem, letting her response dictate my own. To almost every question she asked—"Are you going to break it off?" or "Are you going to keep on doing this?"—I answered, "I don't know."

Janice gave me the ultimatum of giving up my affair or moving out. I had two weeks to make up my mind. She was too mad to try to get to the bottom of what was going on or not going on between us. Later, by the time she had cooled off enough to ask me to see a marriage counselor, I no longer cared what happened to our marriage; I could conveniently remind her of the time I had asked her to go with me to a counselor and she had refused.

Had my affair only been a booster for my libido and ego, I probably would have come to "my senses" and vowed at the end of the two weeks to mend my tattered character through a long probation. But that would have required a feeling of guilt on my part, and I had none.

I had fallen in love. It was a rosy sensation not too far removed from the religious longing I had had at age twelve, and so I felt holy in it. The strength of it transformed my guilt into historical necessity; I might have been able to renounce a desire for sexual variety, but I couldn't let go of what, it seemed to me, I had been truly looking for in a mate without quite being conscious of it. Not having had real intimacy in my marriage, I had been stunned to understand for the first time how close two people could become and precisely what that felt like.

Marcia and I had begun as two coworkers, then we

worked our way through daily contact to chatting ac-
quaintances, from there to lunches where we talked—
sometimes about our trying marriages—and learned mutual trust, and ascended from there to flirtations at parties,
inevitably wound up in bed, then shortly thereafter in love.
After six months, I knew ten times more about this woman
than I had learned about Janice in eighteen years, in no
small part because Marcia was an inveterate talker: She
had come from a family in which no thing went unsaid, be
it helpful or destructive, and she probed me continually
for my true relations to things.

We shared the comfort of mutual knowledge that allows
you to sit in a restaurant and the moment a stranger enters
you know what each will notice about said stranger. When
we were concentrating on one another we were each a
wonder-inspiring encyclopedia for the other's enchanted
perusal, and when we turned our attention to the world,
our perception of it was happily whole, like perfectly focused binoculars. Loving a close friend and being close
friends with the person you love was a devastating combination, and when you added a profoundly magnetic physical attraction, it was inconceivable to me that I could learn
to live without this woman in two decades, let alone two
weeks.

I say I didn't feel guilty about being in love, but that's
not to say I didn't feel guilty about being out of love. One
summer night shortly after Janice's ultimatum, I was on a
business trip to New York. Around midnight, since I couldn't
sleep I turned off a shuddering air-conditioner in my hotel
room and watched a hot rain fall on the streets outside as
I coaxed memories from me of how Janice and I had started
dating.

I had asked Janice out after meeting her through a mutual friend. We were to have a "coffee date," not only

because it would be cheap, but also so that I could talk about myself.

Janice wore jeans and a blouse, and her patrician features were unadorned by makeup. She listened, long fine fingers laced under her chin, as I jabbered nervously. Now and then I braved a glance into those dazzling, undefinable eyes, wondering what she was thinking. Chain-smoking, I raved about Sartre and Camus and Heidegger, logical positivism and Heisenberg's Uncertainty Principle. She could not have known what I was talking about because I myself didn't, but I was impressed by how seriously she took me, though she was not flirtatious. Her attentive silences awed me, and I thought here was a beauty with brains—she could name the authors of books she had read—who willingly endured my attentions.

For two months we dated. I wrote poetry for her, to her. I read poetry she had written and graded it. Around Thanksgiving, we had a spat. To complete our breakup, I decided to take her toaster from my apartment, where we were casually and unofficially cohabiting, back to her dorm room. As I delivered it, I heard myself ask her to marry me.

We were still undergraduates, I barely over twenty-one, she not quite twenty. We had no jobs, and were two years from graduation. What was our hurry? If I had returned the toaster and simply said good-bye, then we would have been just another young couple caught momentarily in a billow of romance that collapsed quickly.

The hurry? I wanted to be married. Janice was the fourth woman I had been in love with since age seventeen, and I was tired of the turmoil of courtship. I believed in the Fifties concept of marriage as the blissful arrival of stasis after the teeth-rattling carnival ride of romance. You got married and the movie of your life dissolved into end credits and swells of music. From then on, you never had to worry about getting a partner or agonizing over the relationship. You could get on with the more important stuff: what to do, what to be.

Janice said yes for much the same reason. Also, having a church wedding in her hometown only months after her public humiliation—she and her original intended groom had aleady sent out wedding announcements when she discovered he had another fiancée elsewhere—must have seemed an attractive way to save face.

I remembered how we got a small furnished apartment, bought some Joan Baez records and became newlyweds. ("Did you come, huh? Did you, huh, huh?") We worried about school, about our future careers, about money, we ate hotdogs and mashed potatoes and watched TV on a tiny black-and-white set. I gained ten pounds and Janice got gynecological infections. I worked weekends as a musician, and Janice got a part-time job as a hostess at a restaurant. For six months we played house blissfully.

But her friends were actors and dancers; mine were political radicals. After a while I began to feel our differences as sharp pains. Occasionally she would want to attend church, and that would drive me into fits of embarrassment as deep and irrational as a teenage boy's shame over a beat-up family car. My conception of marriage had been formed by my parents' life. They never argued in front of the children; they seemed almost precisely alike to me, barring differences of gender. I never imagined that marriage meant having to struggle over mutually exclusive personal preferences.

So, when I was about to go off to my annual Marine Corps Reserve camp the first summer after we were married, I told Janice, out of the blue, that I wanted her to be moved out of our apartment when I got back. I didn't give her an explanation, because I really didn't have one. Had I looked too closely at myself, I would have seen a person in Marine Corps fatigues claiming that his wife was not sufficiently radical to suit his friends.

While I was gone, I realized I had acted absurdly and couldn't imagine what had possessed me. When I returned, Janice had moved most, but not all, of her possessions out of the apartment.

"What are you doing? You really don't have to go, I was just being silly," I said, like someone surprised at being taken seriously when a joke had been intended.

That rainy August night in New York, it seemed to me that I had mistreated her for eighteen years, making decisions about her life, dragging her here and there across the country, only to heap on top of this abuse the last, most damaging blow—leaving her.

*You're lonely, are you? Whose fault is that? Take a good hard look!* Until now, I had been content to be self-contained, but suddenly my self wasn't such an attractive container to be trapped inside of.

I could see now that when I was young I felt threatened by intimacy, so I had picked a mate who wouldn't intrude on my privacy. I had protected this "privacy" only to discover in my late thirties that it had soured into loneliness. I blamed my condition on Janice, even though I had created it.

I had many ways of keeping out of reach. All my methods stemmed from the premise that to concede to a wife's request to do something that runs counter to your interests or convictions is a sign of weakness. I wouldn't have endorsed that publicly, though I acted as if I believed it. But what I thought of as strength was really a fear of intimacy: If I had done something she'd asked me to do even when she knew I didn't want to do it, it would've shown her I cared for her.

"Why don't you take me dancing?" she would ask.

"Because I don't like to dance. I spent so many years as a musician watching dancers from a bandstand that I just see them as annoying drunks making buffoons of themselves, and besides, music is supposed to be listened to," I'd say. I meant *It's beneath my dignity; I'm not an audience, I'm an artist!* Also, this reminded her that when we met she was a frivolous air-head who belonged to an Arthur Murray exhibition dance group, and by marrying me she had been spared a lifetime of intellectual sterility.

But even this subterranean message was not really to the point. There was more to it. When I had begged her to come back to me after we were separated in graduate school, I had said, "I'll even learn to do the tango," and after she came back I allowed her to try to teach me on our kitchen floor with the steps chalked out, but it felt like some strange club-footed cakewalk at a frenetic pace. I was too clumsy and stupid, I said, to do it. But I promised to try. Once I got her securely back into the fold, however, I reneged by always having the proverbial headache. It's how I punished her for making me humiliate myself to get her back.

*Do you want to dance?*

*No, thank you.*

The subtext is unreadable to outside parties, and even we were, in a way, outside parties. Not even I knew all that I meant by saying no. Did she realize when she asked that I was only hearing *Show me you love me?*

That night, sitting by the window, I bawled. I was floored by remorse and guilt, not only for how badly I had treated Janice then but how, when she came back, I had led her down the garden path for almost two decades and was

93

about to drop her hand again at the edge of a precipice. I grieved to realize that whatever love I had had for her was gone; I was furious with myself for no longer loving her, because no longer loving her meant that all those years she had invested in me had come to a bad end, abruptly. I wept out of anger that I couldn't make myself have the feelings I *wanted* to have—I wanted to have the choice of loving Janice, but I didn't have it. Loving her would have made everything in my life very simple, clean, uncluttered. Above all, it would have prevented anyone from getting hurt.

Finally I shut the window, but it rained all night.

And what about the kids?

They had eased to the back of my mind. They were now in fourth grade, seemed happy and thriving, had friends in the neighborhood, seemed totally oblivous to the tension between their mother and father, whose discussions about their future were carried on after midnight in hissed whispers.

But during the grace period in which I was supposed to resolve my conflicts, Keith and Nicole shot suddenly into the foreground of my attention. It was inconceivable to me that I could give up the woman I loved. But it was also inconceivable that I could leave the children I loved.

The two were mutually exclusive alternatives. But I thought that if I gnawed at the knot long enough, eventually I'd undo it; I'd find a solution that would be best for everyone. However, I wasn't willing to look the problem in the eye and confess my weakness and failure; I had to find a way to make my most desired outcome acceptable to myself. I very carefully constructed a mental portrait of my future life in which my children were perfectly satisfied having my complete attention during scheduled visitations, as opposed to having my perfunctory attention in and around a daily routine. Quality of time was what was important, I told myself, not the quantity of it. It seemed simple, then: All I had to do was to vow to spend high-quality time with my children after I moved out and that would provide adequate compensation for their loss. I had taken pride in being a good father, I knew, so that was money in the bank. I had given them much more of me than fathers usually give, so they wouldn't turn against me, would they?

One afternoon during my two-week grace period, I was cooking spaghetti sauce. The kitchen was hot, so I escaped into the living room while the sauce was simmering. I was thinking about getting through this meal, getting the kitchen cleaned up, going out to meet Marcia later on. Now that I had confessed to Janice, I had no need to lie about where I was going.

Outside, the air was sticky and hot. The kids were playing in the front yard with a neighbor's boy. They were in swimsuits and were taking turns spraying one another with the garden hose. My kids were brown from having spent much of their summer either at camp or at their granparents' lake houses; their hair was shaggy, sun-bleached, and the soles of their feet were tough as dried cowhide. Nicole wore a one-piece suit in a Day-Glo chartreuse. At nine, she had long thin limbs, shoulder blades like the hard, hairless wings of just-born birds; she had lost her baby-belly, and her small hard butt cheeks looked like muscle under her wet suit. She was still in the tom boy, tree-climbing stage, but I was conscious of her gender, how she was one and the boys were two, how her suit was different from theirs. When she controlled the hose, she'd hold the spray so that it arced like a rainbow over the sidewalk, and she'd scream at the boys to run under it. Or she'd hold it steady so that the stream shot up like a fountain and came back down like rain, and she kept trying to get the boys to stand under it with her.

This wasn't warlike enough for Keith. When he grabbed the hose from her, he tried to squirt her in the face, but she ran off. She and their friend would then dash to the circumference of the hose's reach, mug and taunt him, and he would try to spray them. They would pretend they didn't want to be sprayed; he would stalk them while they stood still then rush at them with the hose, making a machine-gun sound, and they would yelp and run out of reach. But then, needing to be cooled off, they'd come back within reach and "accidentally" let him drill them with the spray. What was this game, where the object was to not get wet when getting wet was the object of the game? They were learning to pretend to not want what they really wanted; they were learning to make what someone else wants something you can pretend to punish them with by giving. This was the dance of disguised motives, hiding your pleasures.

They hardly knew they were learning what they would soon need. They were hardly conscious of the adult world; they felt so safe so far under it, for there was that big buffer of several years between themselves and adulthood. They were not even teenagers yet. They lived in a fog of childhood so dense and so omnipresent that they had not even conceived that something now invisible lay beyond it. Maybe thay knew kids in school whose parents were divorced; maybe they knew what that meant and maybe they didn't. Maybe they had no inkling that it meant that both your parents didn't live with you at the same time, and maybe they did. Maybe they did and had been thinking, *Oh, I'm glad that hasn't happened to me, won't happen to me.* And if I left them, it would be happening to them and they would learn so dreadfully early that whatever is bad out there can, indeed, happen to you. And, worse yet, they would learn that I, the father they loved, would be the bad that happened, and it would not be an accident or something I *had* to do—no, their Daddy would be leaving them because he *wanted* to live somewhere else, with someone else.

*They're playing now; tomorrow their lives will be different but they don't know it, now.* I hated my foreknowledge; it was too easy to see their present good spirits and their innocent unawareness of trouble as the last bubbling of childhood. Tomorrow would bring the pain that marks the separation of one age from another. Would it be shocking to them? Janice and I had hardly ever fought between ourselves, let alone in front of them. Any news that Daddy and Mommy are "not getting along" will come without much preparation.

I left the living-room window and went to stir the sauce. Would they miss my spaghetti? I went into Nicole's bedroom. I had painted the walls, the woodwork, the chest of drawers. I had put shelves in the closet. I was the only one tall enough to change the bulb in the overhead fixture. I could make her record player work when the switch on the lid was on the blink. I had given her a pride of stuffed animals that lined her bookshelves and lay in a herd, asleep on her unmade bed. I would not be here to recite her goodnight poem—"Good night / Sleep tight / Wake up bright in the morning light / To do what's right with all your might"—or to read *Curious George* aloud. I would not be here to fix the flat on her bike, to watch her do a trick with a baton or to fix Barbie's leg.

The sadness of it weighed on me and I sat on the bed with my head in my hands. I cursed myself. At that moment, what I wished for most intensely was that I loved Janice and that Janice loved me as much as I wanted and needed to be loved. Then none of this suffering would be necessary. But it wasn't so, would not be so. I couldn't wish myself into the condition of love. I had already tried to wish myself *out* of love with the woman who later that night I would meet, later next year would live with, later still would marry. Love absolutely refused to come and go at my convenience.

Before long I was thinking about how I could get an apartment and cook spaghetti for the kids, how I could have them on weekends (I knew that I would be staying with them every weekend so long as their mother had her present job, anyway), how we'd go to their soccer games, piano lessons, PTA meetings just as always. They had only to give me a ring and I'd come running. I'd be just minutes away; I had been farther away then that when I had the fellowship at the ranch and they had survived quite nicely, hadn't they? Really, the more I thought about it, the more it seemed likely that they might not even notice the difference between my staying and "leaving," such as it was; I simply wouldn't be *sleeping* here any more, and since they were unconscious themselves in sleep, they'd hardly know I wasn't around. When you got right down to it, there was nothing to prevent me from being as good a father as I had been, it was only a matter of careful scheduling. Right?

I clung fiercely to this idea that my leaving wouldn't matter because I really would not be absent. That made it acceptable to me to leave Janice. How it would be possible to somehow be present for the children yet absent for their mother I didn't ask.

Near the end of the two-week period, Janice asked me what my decision was. I said I didn't know, that I hadn't made one.

"Are you going to keep on having an affair?" she asked.

"Yes."

"Then get out."

I had taken the coward's way out of letting the decision be hers to make rather than mine. Who could blame her for giving me the boot? Janice's cold mastery of the situation made everything seem inexorable. Well, I thought, this is just an experiment. I went hunting and located a furnished one-bedroom apartment about fifteen minutes away. I planned to move in over the next weekend; in the meantime, I could stay in my studio downtown for a few days.

Janice and I had agreed, I thought, to ameliorate the shock and damage to the kids by maintaining a spirit of mutual cooperation. We were going to tell them that this was only a trial separation, which, to my mind, was either the truth or a lie, depending on what mood I was in. The day we decided they'd be told, I presumed we'd sit them down in the living room and break the news, over their heads, together. The words would come hard, I knew, because every speech I composed ahead of time sounded lame and false, and I couldn't seem to frame any phrase that would make my leaving a necessity that would outweigh any claim they might have on me. But, as their father and the parent who had chosen to go, it was my duty to speak; the words were rightfully mine, and the difficulty of saying them would be part payment for my guilt. Facing them while I said whatever I would say was both manly and fatherly.

But when I pulled into the driveway late that afternoon after work, they were huddled together at the curb, looking stricken, two nine-year-olds waiting for the Dachau bus. They didn't run up to the car when I stopped—did they know something was up? "Hello, monkeys!" I yelled out. "Hello, Daddy," Nicole said in a small, earnest voice, but Keith wouldn't look my way.

99

At the front door I knocked on the screen. It seemed strange—hours before the house had belonged to me. I went inside to say that I was taking the kids to eat before we had our talk.

Janice said she had walked with them down to a nearby park, where she told them we were going to separate. "I hope you don't mind," she offered politely. "After all, it's our problem now." *So you go on about your merry way and don't bother about us!*

Yes, I *did* mind—it's one thing to confess you're a scumbag and another to have the news precede your appearance. Obviously, part of my punishment would be to be denied any strategy I might devise for my absolution, however meager. I had been undercut here in an unsettling way. It would take me months to dope it all out, but looking back I would pinpoint this as the first moment in a very long series of events when my carefully constructed notions of what could and would happen to my children as a result of my actions were jarred by an unexpected reality.

I could picture the three of them at the park, Janice telling them about me, about our separation, a little as if she were reporting that I had died and that they would have to go on without me. She had deliberately cut me out of the scene; she obviously felt she had the right to control what they heard about us and instinctively knew that for the rest of their lives they would never forget how I was not present at that moment. I had not realized how in leaving the three of them I was giving over so much of my authority to her. Or, rather, that I would lose it.

"How'd they take it?" It infuriated me that I had no way of knowing except through her report.

"Okay," she said. "Considering."

I slunk back to my car. Keith and Nicole were already in it. Nicole sat in the front seat. Gray coils of mud were

*100*

clinging to the rims of her tennis shoes. I almost told her to get out and wipe off her shoes but didn't, not because it would have seemed petty in juxtaposition with the news about my leaving but because I had, in one stroke, lost my moral authority.

We went to Burger King, White tile, hard plastic benches, everything colored in the hues of chewable vitamins. Across from us sat four elderly women in hair nets. We ate food out of cartons; something was wedged between steam-warmed buns that felt damp to the touch; the fries were the size and texture of a whittler's shavings—fries for the occasion. We were all bolting from the silence by stuffing our mouths with anything handy. It was the first of a thousand dreary fast-food meals with just the two of them.

"So what do you think?" I finally asked.

Keith shrugged, which I interrupted to mean indifference or stoic acceptance. Now I know he felt helpless, numb and utterly confused.

"Just a separation," said Nicole.

"Yes," I said, "just a separation." A legalistic truth: I was ninety-nine percent certain we would be divorced, but that remaining one percent permitted me the luxury of cowardice. "I'll see you all the time," I added. "I won't go away." This I truly wanted to believe.

Nobody had an appetite. I sat stewing with frustrations and anxieties I still feel, six years later. Being shut out of how they were told and arriving after the fact; having to rely on hearsay as to how they reacted; feeling guilty and impotent to discipline them (later Keith would say, "I don't have to mind you any more. You don't live here!"); feeling that I had plummeted to the bottom of the pecking order, where my children could now make me grovel to be forgiven; and, finally, feeling weighted with this industrial-strength sadness that we would never be a family again.

That night flipped everything on its ear—I was their father, but I could not protect them because *I* was the threat, I could not guide them because I had lost the right.

I couldn't make myself talk about anything important, and that also discouraged talking about anything inconsequential—it would have seemed vulgar. *The* subject sat on the table between us like a Venus flytrap the size of a basketball we were each pretending was only a private hallucination.

Not knowing what to say, I was unpleasantly surprised by a growing sense of relief that Janice had already "explained" it to them. I asked "How was school?" and "Did you do your homework?" knowing that no child in his right mind could perform any productive work after having heard such crushing news.

"How about some ice cream?"

They shook their heads. Nicole was near tears.

"Aw, come on, surely you want some ice cream?"

Surely you won't hate me for the rest of your life?

# SIX

## Uncle Dad

I took my stereo, guitar, typewriter, books and a few household necessities and moved into my new digs.

I also brought with me items I had collected over the years at flea markets: a telescoping metal cup, a razor that folded into a zippered purse no bigger than my palm, a break-away toothbrush. I had thought I'd bought them out of admiration for their ingenious engineering, but now, toting them off in a shoebox, I understood that they were precisely what a fastidious hobo might stow away in the pockets of a greatcoat. I must have known someday I would be traveling light.

Everybody said fellows got taken to the cleaners on the house, the lawn chairs, how everything down to the canned goods was signed over to the rejected spouse in the settlement—there was even a bumper sticker that said MY EX-WIFE GOT THE BMW. But I didn't covet hedge clippers or welcome mats or any of the hernia-inducing golden oak antiques I had labored to restore, and that went double for framed posters, carpets, knickknacks, or what-nots and their silly little shelves. These things meant nothing now; had Keith not already broken them I could have given him those precious chess pieces to do with what he wished. It comforted me to think I wasn't removing any significant fixtures from their lives—myself notwithstanding.

Get-away tunes hummed in my head. "Hit the Road, Jack." I sang about the other Jack, who went out the back, and the Stan who made a new plan. I was curiously elated, as if I were going off to college or to camp for the first time. But my secret glee disturbed me; not only was it unseemly to show it, but *feeling* this inappropriate sense of liberation, rather than remorse, proved I was a scumbag.

The aforementioned digs were in an old Mediterranean-style building in the city's anemically bohemian district. It was reputed to have been the residence of the man who penned "Home on the Range" in the 1930s, the decade from which the furniture and smelly mattresses doubtless dated. The wooden window blinds were held in place by rotting strips of fabric; to give them a sorely needed vacuuming would be to risk having them disintegrate in my hands. Otherwise, the building was fairly clean but run-down, with a certain old-world charm. The facade sported arabesque curlicues hanging under the red tile roof and plaster columns twisted like Christmas candy along the front porch; at the back of the hallway stood an elevator the size of a refrigerator with an accordioned door of brass bars that made large gold diamonds when you pulled it across the opening. The kids'll love this, I thought.

The place had "atmosphere" and "character," but I never defined this ambience very precisely, perhaps for good reason. There were twelve apartments, all furnished, all cheap; except for the gay couples above and below me, each contained a lone occupant. But this was not swinging Singlesville; everybody here was ugly, old, broke, and/or in deep spiritual difficulty. A bear-shaped middle-ager on the top floor worked as a clown at children's birthday parties and kept a parrot in his rooms; my nearest neighbor was a fat girl who wore hiking boots and plaid shirts and threatened to join the Navy. Neither of the two gay male couples had any taste whatsoever in interior decorating. A helmet-haired spinster in her fifties who worked as an accountant once bravely held a party for the building, but everybody was so scared it would be a grim gathering that they took extra care not to show up at once. She wound up holding painfully stiff conversations with a thin trickle of neighbors, the way it is when somebody dies and people bring casseroles to pay their respects. In retrospect, I think I must have sensed I was moving into a House of Cripples. The undercurrent of hopelessness must have been alluring—to live here was to seat myself among the ashes of the hearth for absolution.

First, though, I had to pass muster by the owner, the osteoporadic widow of an oil man. She and a traveling companion tooled around the state in an ancient green Packard checking on her properties. She wore dark calf-length dresses and thick-heeled lace-up shoes, chastised her hair with a tight bun and peered suspiciously at me through wireless glasses during the interview in the downstairs apartment she reserved for her own use. Mrs. Hurford asked me if I drank. "Socially," I said. I had on a tie. Interviewing to live here was absurd—drug deals went down in the alley—but I was rushing to dump myself somewhere and thus had to endure this formality. Mrs. H. obviously had no real knowledge of the neighborhood and was perhaps trying to protect a genteel reputation for the building that persisted only as an anachronism in her mind.

She asked where I had been living. I put on my teacher-preacher face and said that my wife and I were trying a temporary separation. I worked at looking aggrieved, as if I might say more about my wife were I not a gentleman. This low tactic brought out Mrs. Hurford's maternal instincts, although no sooner had I written a check for the deposit than she said, "Your children won't be living with you, of course." I said that they would be with me on the weekends. "Well," she said slowly, "this has always been a very quiet building." I assured her I would maintain control. I felt hypocritical, but Mrs. H.'s concern was laughable. I was having to pretend my own standards were far more rigorous than they actually were so that I could be admitted into the company of sodomites and coke-snorters. The first thing I planned to do upon entering this select crowd was to call Marcia and, if her husband didn't answer the phone, invite her over to make the slobbering beast with two backs in my saggy bed.

Keith and Nicole helped me to move. They burst through the downstairs door, pushed all the buzzers by the mailboxes, played chase in the hall, rattled the elevator doors and shouted to each other up the stairwell. I wanted them to feel at home, but their footfalls pounding in the hallway made me cringe. I gave them dresser drawers for storing books, puzzles, games and some extra underwear and socks. On overnighters, they slept together in an old Murphy bed in the living room. They liked the concept of a pull-down bed far greater than they liked sleeping in it; they fought over covers, and the sag sent them rolling into the middle so they gouged one another with their elbows and knees all night.

"Where's your TV, Dad?" asked Keith.

"I don't have one."

He looked alarmed. "Are you going to get one?"

"Maybe," I said. It took a week to decide the issue. I considered not getting one because I had always detested the sound of Saturday morning cartoons. Whenever I'd see the kids watching "animated" figures jerk spastically while uttering stupid dialogue in high-pitched voices, I'd feel as if all civilization were being crushed, right in my living room, under the heel of a spiritually bereft technology. I hated abetting it. The way Keith cozied up to the set had always alarmed me. He was nearsighted but didn't like to wear his glasses, so he'd sit or lie within arm's reach of the set, close enough that the colored light spilling from it would bathe his form in eerie hues. Unlike Nicole, who got bored with it after a half hour or so, Keith could spend eight hours entranced by the screen, drool dripping down his chin. When you broke up the magnetic connection between his attention and the tube, he'd be cranky.

At first I thought that when they came over we'd talk, play games, do projects, cook, listen to music. If they needed entertainment, they could read comic books or I'd read stories to them. My life would be a testament to doing quite well without things you imagined were essential; a living museum of a time before TV when talk was paramount. God knows I needed to think *something* was admirable about my life.

But Keith kept asking, "Are you going to get a TV?" It became clear that *if I didn't have a TV he wouldn't want to come to my apartment.* This was terrifying. Sure, I could make him come, but I couldn't make him enjoy it, couldn't make him *want* to come, and if he ceased to want to come, he would cease to love me, I thought.

I was entering the Twilight Zone of the Divorced Dad. Should you do things for your children that you think aren't good for them merely because they want them? Of course not, most normal parents would say. But the divorced parent has had his (or her) common sense crippled by guilt. Having "abandoned" my son, it seemed "wrong" to deny him anything that was in my power to give; it seemed obligatory to make him as comfortable as possible under the circumstances (as if he were sick, or dying). It seemed "wrong" to deny him something even if it was against my convictions that he should have it, because, for one thing, I didn't trust my convictions; my self-esteem was low, and all my judgments seemed tainted.

I couldn't afford a TV. But scraping up the money by making sacrifices made the purchase not only morally acceptable, it made it imperative. "He can barely pay his rent after child support," I imagined someone saying, "but he bought that television just so his boy could watch it when he came to visit." Playing the martyr made it seem I hadn't created these conditions myself, had had them cast upon me instead. And oh how these old conflicts can still dog me: Now, as I write this, Keith is fifteen, soon to be sixteen, living in my home. He attends a private preparatory school where the student parking lot is filled with automobiles that put my battered Chevy to shame. Should I buy a new car so he won't be embarrassed by my old one, even though I don't believe I actually need one and even though I don't believe that cars should be taken seriously as symbols of status? Should I adhere to an inferior set of values for the sake of allowing him to feel secure in a world of them? Or shouldn't I stand for something better? (I say yes, and I *am* tougher these days.)

Janice filed for divorce so quickly it made me wonder whether she hadn't been looking for an excuse—hers was a smoking pen—and as the fall inched by, our lawyers hammered out the arrangements, taking their cues from us. Or did we take our cues from them? She got the house and most of the contents, the newer car, and for a time my lawyer told me that she wanted fifty percent of the future sales of rights to books I had already written or was writing. This didn't sound like her to me—it had the stench of lawyerly bluster—but I had to take it seriously.

Then there was custody. I knew very little about custody arrangements and hadn't bothered to investigate, since looking into it would require admitting that what I was doing could have unpleasant permanent consequences for my children and me.

In most other cases, daddies moved out and the kids stayed with mommy. This traditional resolution to divorce, with the father departing from the home and sending back support checks, was the natural, *extraordinary* expression of his *ordinary* status within the family; this departure was akin to all his other daily departures and absences except in one significant aspect.

But Janice and I had shared the parenting; we had both worked and both stayed home, and, except for the year at the ranch, I had been unusually present as a father hour by hour around the hearth. I thought we should both continue to be important to the kids and to divvy the chores. Joint custody, something I'd not heard of, came to my attention. I knew a fellow who lived a couple of blocks away from his ex, and their daughter alternated weeks with each parent.

When I proposed joint custody to Janice through the lawyers, she turned it down, to my amazement. She wanted sole custody, with visitation rights only for me. Although she later said, "I was afraid I would lose them, too," at the time this wholly unprecedented show of maternal ferocity looked like spite. An unexpected fear rushed to mind: With sole custody, could she whisk my children off to a distant city without my consent? The saddest men were those whose children were literally out of reach, and I had one friend who arrived at his children's home one day to find it empty, with no fowarding address left.

What could I do to force joint custody? In our state, at this time, not much. The courts wouldn't award joint custody unless Janice agreed to it. (It has since become easier for fathers to achieve it even over the spouse's objections.) And nothing could prevent her from moving them away, either, my lawyer told me. "It'd be a good idea to stay on friendly terms," he said.

Was I angry? Well, I pretended to be. I wanted desperately to believe that I wanted joint custody. In truth, I wanted to see the kids when I wanted to, wanted to feel as if I were their father and to have them acknowledge that I still was. I wanted my normal say in where they went to school, who their dentists and doctors and pals were, how they spent their leisure time and who they spent it with. I was loath to relinquish any of the authority I was long accustomed to exercising over their lives.

But I really didn't want them constantly underfoot. Despite the squalor of my apartment, I was having the time of my mid-life and didn't want my fun to be spoiled by heart-broken children who hung around asking questions that were too difficult for me to ask myself, let alone answer. Nothing I admit to in these pages shames me more than this.

For the several months while Janice worked weekends, Keith and Nicole spent time in my apartment. On Saturday mornings, I'd rise and try to work at the kitchen table, giving over my bed for them to lie in and to watch cartoons, the sounds of which bounced around the apartment while I worked. Now and then they would get up to peer out of my bedroom window; it had a view onto an alley where the wan, androgynous denizens of a unisex hair boutique met during break-time to compare rainbow-colored hair and to pass a joint, and sometimes each other's tongues, among them; I was cursed with the fear that my folly had unwittingly led my pink-cheeked babes out of innocence much too soon.

In cold weather, we stayed inside to play Monopoly on a carpet so old that cross-hatched twine showed through burgundy fuzz. If the weather was nice, I would walk them down to a nearby park to play Horse with a spongy basketball; we went bowling, we went to movies, we went roller-skating, ice-skating, we haunted video arcades.

Suddenly my role was shifting. As a normal father, I had usually spent my weekends maintaining a home and overseeing my children's activities—helping a little here, chatting a little there, giving a scruff on the head while, say, passing a passel of kids who were setting up a Hot Wheels track on the front porch. But now I had become an entertainment director, an insecure one at that, who had to keep his charges engaged every second in some frenetic, mind-numbing activity, because if we were suddenly to come to a halt with nothing to do, the moment would be a vacuum into which our mutual sadness was sure to rush. I had to be jolly every minute they were with me—how could they not love a guy who tried so hard to please them? Every weekend became a 48-hour birthday party, and my grades as a father depended entirely on bringing them "home" exhausted and happy, even if it sorely taxed my budget and made them tired almost to tears.

Now when I took my kids to the zoo, I noticed other fathers without partners and instantly knew their story. We could distinguish each other from the regular, full-time dads merely giving mom a break because they were allowed to look bored. When I took them to a G-rated movie on a Saturday afternoon, single parents would be the only adults in the audience—you could see their heads sticking up here and there down the rows like large cabbages in a rank of beets—and I'd think *There's another Uncle*

*Dad trying to get through the day,* because regular fathers just sent their kids there. In fast-food joints, I'd notice men sitting alone over cold pizza and staring into space while their charges played video games. To me, our visibility made eating in public painful. Sometimes I saw a woman at an Uncle Dad's table who was obviously not the children's mother; she was acting as a beard to keep people from thinking this was not a normal family.

We weren't "normal" fathers; when our kids went out with us, they were guests—the way it might be when an uncle came to town on a semiannual junket, bearing slightly inappropriate gifts and showering his nephews and nieces with attentions for a few hours before vanishing back into his own life. At times I thought that some shrewd entrepreneur might do well to build an Uncle Dadland, a sort of parents-without-partners theme park where we could feel comfortable. The electricity for the place could be generated by huge round cages in which the Uncle Dads could run like hamsters to work off their guilt. If that venture seemed too costly or ambitious, maybe we could have an Uncle Dad's Fried Chicken franchise where we wouldn't have to face, and envy, that wholesome family with a full contingent of parents seated across the aisle from us, where we wouldn't feel we had neon signs attached to our heads anouncing that we're from a Broken Home.

To avoid such embarrassment and because it was cheaper, I usually cooked for the kids at my apartment. Concocting an *Uncle Dad's Cookbook* also occurred to me, though no recipe I could give would sound appealing to anybody but an orphan raised on institutional food. I made dispirited Sunday dinners of boiled wieners and the old favorite, Kraft macaroni and cheese. This was not the extent of my cooking vocabulary, but I couldn't locate any inspiration to do better, and I felt the kids were too impatient and restless to sit in the apartment while I cooked. I missed my old utensils—it's amazing how you take something as simple as a colander for granted. One morning I fixed a poached egg on toast, which had been my usual breakfast fare for years, and offered one to Nicole, but she slowly shook her had. "Those eggs make me sad," she said.

Janice wasn't off on Sunday nights until ten, so I'd take the kids home after supper to give them time to unwind, bathe and be in bed by the time she arrived. As I came back into the house I had once owned, my eye would alight on all my former objects now put in new places. I couldn't bring myself to enter the bedroom. I would notice burned-out bulbs, doors that wouldn't shut, bubbles in the kitchen linoleum, clothes that needed washing, dripping faucets that needed new washers. After I put the kids to bed, I would sit in the old rocking chair which years ago had been a gift from a woman, a mutual friend, who had come to stay with us, in another house, in another state, in another time of crisis, that one hers. I would sit as close to the front door as I could get and resist the urge to go about fixing things. The signs of neglect reproached me. I couldn't blame Janice for not maintaining things—the kids told me she spent many hours in the bathroom, crying. Sometimes I'd succumb, find a screwdriver and reset the screws in a door hinge or replace a bulb in an overhead fixture, hoping, as I did, that Janice wouldn't notice so she wouldn't think I still cared, and then hoping that she would notice so she'd know how much she had needed me and would regret her loss. Sometimes I did repairs because it used to be my house and I hated to see these things go undone; more often I did them because I didn't want my children to grow up in a house that looked neglected, because if it did the world would know whom to blame.

I'd try to read until I saw the lights of a car in the driveway, then, because I couldn't stand being with Janice inside this house I'd bolt out the door, bound down the steps and into my own car, performing a changing of the guard with a mere salute.

During the week, I would drive Nicole to a nearby town for gymnastics lessons; two afternoons a week, I took Keith to his soccer practice or to games. I shuttled them to their pediatrician and their dentists, chatted with them over the phone, went to PTA meetings and programs, talked with their teachers. These little acts, once the casual gestures of day-to-day life, became the way I earned my merit badges. I kept thinking that if I pressed myself on them, if I refused to give them any room to feel abandoned, then surely they'd keep on loving me. I wanted to believe that I was a good father, even from across town. I even imagined that I had become a better dad, more attentive, more concerned, more focused on them; I consoled myself with the notion that this high-quality time was better for them than merely having me hovering about absent-mindedly.

But real dads provide for, protect and guide their children.

As for providing—well, Janice had a job that paid much more than mine, and my child support payments might, on a lean month, cover their mortgage and food. Even as thriftily as I was living, I had reduced their circumstances. I was no longer a primary provider.

Protecting them? Now they were latch-key kids. One day they arrived home from school to discover the front door yawning open on a splintered frame, and they impulsively stepped across the glass shards to inspect their rooms for missing possessions. They had been burglarized, I learned that night. When I heard how they had gone into the house, I thought, My God! What if the burglar were still there? I tried to tell myself that even had I been living there I probably wouldn't have been home when it had all happened anyway. This potential disaster could also have befallen the children of a married dad, but the rationalization was no comfort—living away from them, I had absolutely no chance of being there.

From then on, it was easy to imagine, when I woke up alone, how some man, who perhaps knew the father was absent from my children's home, might ease open a window some night and enter to do whatever he wished to them. I could imagine how they might be aroused by a noise however harmless and lie awake thinking that no one was home to protect them, no one stood between them and an intruder except their mother. I could picture them in their beds, unable to call "Daddy!" because it would do no good.

Janice had always been fatalistic about security, having grown up in a small town where people left their doors unlocked; sometimes she would leave the newspapers on the walk for days, and when the locks on the doors went on the blink, they went unmended. She kept a spare front door key under a pot on the porch, but when that was lost, the kids crawled in through a bedroom window kept open for that purpose. They'd leave the removed screen standing in the flower-bed, and each time I'd come by to pick them up I'd reset it in the sill. To me, this laxness was tantamount to putting up a sign that read BURGLARS AND RAPISTS ENTER HERE! EASY ACCESS!

At times I wondered if Janice invited assault as a means of making me feel sorry for having been responsible for it; I'd be furious at her for running such risks to make such a point, but then in more level-headed moments I could see that she was as depressed as she was angry (and maybe she felt guilty, also), and this depression had made her apathetic. But always, these signs of my children's new vulnerability made me ache with guilt.

One evening when Janice was working late, Keith climbed onto the roof to rescue a mewling kitten then fell off and struck the air-conditioning unit. While he lay screaming in the driveway, Nicole ran up and down the block trying to find an adult who could help, then phoned for an ambulance herself. A nine-year-old suddenly called upon to be an adult and living up to the unexpected challenge—I could be proud of this, but my normal paternal pride was spoiled by my guilt that my absence had forced this premature maturity on her. I had no right to be proud of any attribute she might develop so long as its origin lay in my neglect.

I learned about the accident twenty-four hours later, when I made an evening call to chat. Nicole related the story. After the ambulance had arrived, Keith had apparently been taken to a nearby emergency room, where he was x-rayed and pronounced essentially undamaged but shaken up.

"Why didn't you call me when it happened?" I asked Nicole. I felt rejected. "I dunno, I just didn't think to," she said helplessly. I think she did know but didn't want to say. *Why call you? You don't live here any more.* When I got Keith on the phone, I said, "I'm glad you weren't seriously hurt." I sounded distant, as if I were, well, an uncle in Massachusetts. "You should be more careful," I added. My words were empty; they came so late from someone so remote that his name could not be usefully conjured during an emergency.

I thought of dozens of safety tips that I had learned over the years and wondered if they had been understood and were being heeded. *Don't use a hair dryer while you're standing in the tub. Don't plug in appliances or touch them while your hands are wet or if you're standing in water. Don't touch the metal prongs of plugs while inserting them into the socket. Don't change a light bulb while the light switch is on. Don't cut into a lamp cord. Don't put any bulb larger than 60 watts into a desk lamp. Don't turn on the gas to a stove burner without striking a match and holding it to the ring first, if the pilot's not working. Don't try to light the gas log in the fireplace without holding a match to the burners before turning on the gas. Don't use an unvented space heater without opening the window a crack for ventilation. Don't try to douse a grease fire by throwing water on it—use baking soda. Don't use gasoline from the lawnmower gas can to clean anything in the house. Don't use the gasoline near an open flame of any kind. Don't play with matches!* (Once it came to my attention that some kids went home with Keith and Nicole after school, and one visitor showed them how to turn an aerosol paint can into a blow torch by lighting the spewing paint.) *Don't run if your clothing catches on fire—roll on the ground. Don't store rags with cleaning fluids or paint or gasoline on them in a closed-up place....* And many, many more.

Had I said these things? Or had I merely lived by them and thought they had been unnecessary to say so long as I was present? Thoughtlessly grabbing a hot pan handle in my own spartan kitchen, I would automatically imagine one of them doing the same when they were alone.

Aside from safety, how about guidance? What could I say to them about the ethics of everyday living that hadn't already been completely undercut by my actions? I learned that one of Nicole's girl friends who had previously spent the night was no longer allowed to since her home was now "broken." I tried to console her. "It's not your fault," I said. "Those are stupid parents, unfair; they're narrow-minded bigots, and you're every bit as good as their daughter!" What might have sounded like common sense coming from my mouth now had the air of special pleading, as if

I were not trying to teach her something about values but instead was simply trying to deny the consequences of my actions.

How could I tell them to consider other people's feelings when I had so obviously ignored theirs? How could I teach them self-denial when I hadn't practiced it? How could I teach them that self-gratification at the expense of another was selfishness? Whatever I might say had a hypocrital stink strong as the odor of a new shower curtain. And they knew it—if I tried to offer advice, they heard it as criticism and reacted by reminding me that I had no ground to stand on.

Along with this divestment of moral authority, I also lost, in their eyes, the right to control their behavior. At first, this wasn't such a problem with Nicole, for she seemed quietly resigned to the divorce. I bought her a nice new dress and took her as my "date" to an awards ceremony in another city, where we danced together at the ball. To make up for her broken home, I got her an intact Barbie Dream House in which Ken and Barbie could live happily with Francie; they had a working toilet and a pink and yellow van to take lots of fun family trips in. Barbie had a wedding dress and they could stay married as long as Nicole wanted her to.

As far as her behavior was concerned, Nicole seemed to be gliding through her days on auto-pilot, so stunned I read her shock as acceptance, and so I managed to ignore the quieter subterranean signs of her distress. She would still listen to an order without arguing about it, though she was quickly learning that since I was not present to enforce any punishment she could blithely ignore me or outflank me by simply going about her own business in a devious way when I was absent.

Keith, however, was erupting in purple, volcanic rages.

Where before the divorce he had been a model child, he was now roaming his neighborhood saying ugly things to adults and pelting their houses with eggs. Mothers who had previously let their sons play with him now thought he was too "wild." His circle of friends shifted from those whose families were intact to other single-parent, latch-key kids like himself who were similarly troubled. Janice and I arranged for group sessions with a family counselor in which Keith's anger was a kind of centerpiece for us to consider, a little as if it were his anger and his reaction to the divorce that needed amending. He refused to talk about anything relating to his feelings; he would braid his arms across his chest and clamp his jaws shut. Everything about his manner said *I'm going to stay mad forever and nobody's going to talk me out of it! There's no use in pretending that I'm the reason we're here—I didn't divorce anybody!* I think he felt it was a grave injustice for the therapist and all of us to attack him for being angry (he saw it as being under attack) when *I* was the one who had behaved badly and wasn't being punished.

His grades tumbled. He told his teachers that when he tried to concentrate, all he could think about was the divorce. I heard this from Janice; she seemed to have an inexhaustible storehouse of these zingers, all of them potent because they were statements of indisputable fact. When she told me about what he had said to his teachers, I could picture the little guy seated at a desk, his brows all gnarled as he stared at cracks in the wood, his head filled with memories of what had been but would never be again, and I knew what might have inspired Kafka to create a man who wakes one morning to discover he's a giant cockroach. What made my guilt especially sharp was that his mother and I, with four degrees between us, had always put a premium on education (my old dreams about their reading *The Odyssey*), and I could remember how, when I was my son's age, the only worry that ruffled my untroubled brow was that my teachers wouldn't like me.

In a snit, he'd decide he wasn't going to school, claim he wasn't feeling well—invariably it would be a Monday morning—and when Janice couldn't force him, they'd quarrel. She would call and tell me to "do something with Keith." He'd be brought to the phone, and if I reproached him or ordered him to do as his mother told him to, he'd say, "I don't have to mind you; you don't live here any more!" He and Nicole had violent fights in which they slapped, kicked, pinched and bit each other and pulled hair, and Janice seemed powerless to stop them. When Keith was verbally abusive to her or when he refused to obey her, Janice would sometimes threaten to call me to come over to spank him if he didn't behave. I was prepared to do this, but it never came to pass, for which I'm grateful: to have barged into their home for that reason would have been adding insult to injury.

Suddenly I was stymied. How can you make someone behave? Looking back on my own childhood, I saw that it hadn't taken much for my parents to keep me in line— my mother gave the orders, my dad stood behind her with his belt ready should a whipping be necessary. I had a child's healthy fear of their authority, and I also wanted their approval. I *accepted* their sovereignty over me. But these were different times, different children, different parents and a much different situation: Divorcing Janice had seriously damaged my children's respect for my authority. It had seriously damaged my *own* respect for my authority, and I could see myself quickly becoming the overly indulgent, fearful, timid and guilt-stricken parent I most feared becoming.

What occurred one late afternoon when I came to take

them to supper is a perfect example of what had begun to happen frequently.

I pulled to the curb after driving through rush-hour traffic to their house. They came bounding out then raced to see who would reach the car first and therefore claim the right to the front seat. Nicole won this time, and this put Keith in a frame of mind to thwart her any way he could.

"So where we going to eat, Dad?" he asked.

"I thought we'd go to Wendy's if that's okay with you guys." I prefered Taco Bueno for food and atmosphere, but I knew they weren't fond of fast-food in the Mexican style. Wendy's has a small selection of more or less edible foods. We'd gone there before and nobody'd complained. From past experience, I'd learned not to ask where they wanted to go; invariably they wouldn't agree, which left me with the swing vote that pleased only one of them.

"Sure," said Nicole.

"I don't want to go to Wendy's," said Keith. "I want to go to Pizza Inn."

He wanted to go to Pizza Inn because he knew Nicole liked Wendy's and because Pizza Inn had video games. Pizza Inn was another few miles down the road through rush-hour traffic, and I knew that if we went there, Keith would spend every minute of his time zapping invaders from space. I felt that we should have some kind of communal intercourse, even if it consisted of nothing more than my asking "How's so-and-so?" and their answering "Fine."

I felt myself getting tense. If I told Keith we weren't going where he wanted to he'd sulk or we'd argue, and the next hour and a half would be a living hell for all. I was afraid to say anything that would upset him, that's how buffaloed he had me. Knowing that he was intimidating me made me angry at myself and at him. I gritted my teeth, vowing to stand up for my own authority. The issue really wasn't one barely palatable bill of fare against another— the issue was, to him, *Do you love me more than you love Nicole? Do you still love me enough to stand up to me?* And, paradoxically, *Do you love me enough to give me my way when I feel I really need it?*

But rather than say, "Tough—it's two against three" or something equally firm and decisive, I said, "I thought you liked Wendy's," in that pleading whine that disgusted me, that sounded as if I was begging him not to make an issue of this. "You never said anything about it last time."

This wasn't a wise tactic, this inviting him to attack my choice from our prior visit.

"Their chili is gross. You and Nicole made me go there. We never go where I want to go."

"We've gone where you want to go plenty of times," I said. "How about if we go next time wherever you want to go?"

"No!" interjected Nicole. "You didn't ask me today where I wanted to go, I just said it was okay to go to Wendy's, but I didn't choose!"

"Well, I'm not going to Wendy's," said Keith. He laced his arms across his chest, flopped back in the rear seat and looked sullenly out his window. I was so furious with him for being such a truculent little shitass that I wanted to pull into the Wendy's lot, drag him bodily inside and force-feed him a bowl of chili with a spoon. Only a small part of my anger came from his defying my authority. A lot more of it came from my frustration and disappointment that this precious time together would be wasted by the stand-off I knew was coming. He'd make sure I understood that the penalty for not indulging him was his withholding his love.

I wanted to bawl. I felt a stinging pressure behind my eyes, but I just clenched my teeth. For a few moments we rode in silence and I thought about whether changing my mind and taking them to Pizza Inn just to make him happy was bad or not. Would it be wish-washy to give in, or was I simply being dogmatic to insist on going to Wendy's? I couldn't see my way through this very clearly. Not being able to decide tempted me to try this other solution on for size. If it turned out to be okay, then perhaps we could have a moderately pleasant time together.

"How do you feel about going to Pizza Inn?" I asked Nicole.

She gave me an absolutely withering look that told me exactly how spineless I was being. "Okay," I chuckled nervously, "Wendy's it is."

"Thanks, Nicole!" screamed Keith. "I'll pay you back later!" By later, he meant when I was no longer around to stick up for her.

Ingeniously, he managed to zing us both in one quick threat. Then I was one hundred percent certain I shouldn't be letting myself be pushed around by a nine-year-old bent on testing me. I was ashamed and mad enough that I no longer cared if he had a tantrum, and I suddenly resigned myself to a spoiled occasion.

"You won't do anything to her for this!" I yelled. "We're going to Wendy's, and that's final. If you want to sit in the car, that's fine. Just act like a baby if you want to."

"You're the one who acts like a baby!" he screamed. This very clumsily shot arrow fell far short of its mark . . . what he meant was that I behaved badly by divorcing his mother.

"Keith, don't talk that way to me!" I warned him. I would've added "I'm your father," but I knew that would only have invited him to deny it.

123

Nicole had closed her eyes, her head lay against the head rest; obviously she was wishing she were somewhere else, as was I.

Keith knew not to push me too far, so he retreated with "I'm not going to wait in the car, either."

"Fine, walk home if you like. It's three miles. The exercise will do you good."

"I'll call Mom. She'll come get me."

He thought this was his most devastating weapon, but I knew Janice wouldn't allow him to play us off against each other.

"Fine."

We parked and Nicole and I went inside. While we were eating, Keith came in with a grin, walked to our table and said, "Give me some money, Dad, so I can get something to eat."

On another occasion similar to this, he might come in, still in a sulk, walk to the table, hold out his hand for money while pointedly looking elsewhere. Or he might stay in the car while we ate. It happened all these ways at one time or another. Another variation on the theme was that he came in with us and waited while we ate then we went through the drive-in at Burger King to get what he wanted. The common denominator here was that our nights out were characterized by quarrels involving me and Keith with the both of us either ignoring Nicole or trying to enlist her as an ally.

After a few months of this, I began to take them out separately, and I found myself wondering why I didn't think of it sooner. For one thing, as soon as she wasn't present, he and I didn't squabble. When he wasn't present, I was free to pay attention to her. Among the many ill effects of the divorce was that their sibling rivalry intensified to a ferociously competitive pitch.

Now, after all these years, I realize what I should have done: When I picked them up together, I should have said. "We're going to Wendy's." None of this "if it's okay with you guys." Or I could have given them a moment to choose between themselves, and if they couldn't agree on his choice of A or hers of B I'd simply choose my own preference, which invariably would be a C that neither had considered. Had I been acting like my usual self, that would have been precisely how I would've handled it.

Because Keith's anger made me angry, often I couldn't see behind it or beyond it. One night, though, late in the spring a few months after I had moved out and the divorce had become final, he and I were driving somewhere, just the two of us, and, out of a pensive silence, he asked, "Dad, do you think that some time I could come live with you?"

"Sure!" I blurted out, without hesitation, pleased to see this show of his regard for me. I immediately felt an onrush of qualms and uncertainties, so I added, "Some time," and then it sounded to my ear as if I were saying "We must do lunch."

"When do you think?" he persisted.

My girlfriend Marcia and I had recently taken a two-bedroom apartment in a duplex over an elderly landlady. We had just set up housekeeping and were learning to be a couple. We kept the second bedroom for Keith and Nicole to use, but I didn't know if the landlady would welcome a child as a permanent addition to my household.

I didn't know if I would, either. I balked at the idea of dealing on a daily basis with my own belligerent, troubled son. It seemed possible, though, that there'd come a time when it could happen, and I didn't want them to grow up without having lived some time with me.

"We'll have to talk about it," I said. "Maybe in the fall."

Putting my own kid off this way made me realize I was a long way from being a good father, and my only consolation was that I was not such cretinous slime as to have walked out of their lives for good. All these failures in providing, protecting and guiding my children prevented my clean escape in some odd, paradoxical way. So long as I could not get an "A" in these aspects of fathering, I felt compelled to try, however hobbled I was by circumstances, for the best grade I could get. I lacked the grit to do what was right, and I was too vain to live with that truth without consoling myself with half measures.

Because I couldn't (or wouldn't) immediately bring him to live with me and Marcia, I bought him a model airplane with a gasoline engine. It was something I had wanted as a kid, and I thought it was good to give him what I had wanted but hadn't had—since I couldn't give him what he wanted—and I wanted to grab a little chunk of my own childhood back this way. "Gee, Dad!" the Beaver (Keith) would gush to Ward (me). "Golly. It flies and it's got a real engine!" Saturdays at the park, little guys and their dads, making machinery go, the smell of fumes, the sputter and whine of engines . . .

I suppose I really hoped it would keep him from noticing I had rejected him a second time. He and I and Nicole went to the park, assembled the plane—it was a kind of break-apart model held together by rubber bands—and got it started. I turned over the control lines to him, but he got dizzy turning on the plane's pivot after a few revolutions. Nicole took a turn, and the plane climbed on a sudden vertical swoop that arced into a loop that took it nosedown into the turf, where it exploded into pieces. I laughed and tried to explain that the plane was built to do that—that was why it was put together with rubber bands in the first place, so it would withstand such a crash—but she burst into tears anyway.

I bought Keith a BB gun to replace the airplane. It was another of my favorite childhood toys. He and a new friend, who had spiked hair and whose parents were also breaking up, chipped a garage window with a shot from the Daisy. The owner called the police and Keith's name went into a computer somewhere. I gave him a feeble lecture, but I knew that I shouldn't have bought the gun for him.

"Keith says you're just trying to buy his love," Janice reported, obviously agreeing.

They were wrong. I was trying to buy his forgiveness.

# SEVEN

# A Lifelike Situation

My diary shows that I was with one or both of my children for 147 days in 1981. They turned eleven that year, went from the fifth to the sixth grade; they were still children enough to enjoy being with parents and to enjoy almost any sort of play, even if it was only fitfully diverting.

I was still driving Nicole to and from piano and gymnastics lessons. During that year, she abruptly gave up her Barbies and became interested instead in school. She was much quieter and more self-contained than Keith, and she was an easier house guest; she could occupy herself by drawing, reading or just piddling, and she would readily agree to activities that Keith would never be interested in. She and I worked several difficult jigsaw puzzles together on the dining room table, and these long, almost wordless hours spent helping each other find the right pieces were mutually pleasurable. We didn't have to talk; sometimes there'd be long, tranquil stretches of silence, and then we'd spontaneously chatter sometimes about things that mattered.

She is athletic and well-coordinated, and liked to ride her bike or go jogging with me. Although she's short, most of her height is in leg, so she had no difficulty running three miles without straining, and I was proud that she could beat me so easily at this. We went skating on a path around a nearby lake; we went bowling—she was usually better than her brother—and when I'd watch in gymnastics class as she put her springy, supple form through a regimen, I would feel happily old. I rejoiced in my children's vigor, energy and good health. This fundamental vitality seemed stronger in them than the domestic trauma they had suffered, and it reassured me that they would heal.

When they were occasionally sick with, say, the flu, they sometimes stayed at my apartment because now I was home mornings and was teaching in the afternoons. They also stayed with us when Janice went away on business, in which case I drove them to school and cooked for them like a normal parent, shelling out lunch money, signing a permission form for a field trip, attending a PTA program or school carnival. That year we went to museums, the circus, the zoo, the Ice Capades, the state fair, the ballet, flea markets, a film festival and the library. We played chess, Pente, Tripoly, gin, Monopoly, Life; we went shopping for clothes and groceries, went trick-or-treating, went to pediatricians and dentists, barbers and beauticians, to the movies, to picnics, to a professional soccer game, to my classes. At home we baked cookies, washed my car, mowed my lawn, mopped floors, polished brass and silver, had birthday parties complete with cake and ice cream and watched the Miss America Pageant.

That summer, I took them on a float trip down the Rio Grande with my parents. I also took them to my parents' lake cottage for several days of swimming and boating, and in the evenings we'd play Yahtzee or a simplified Mah-Jongg.

Keith's anger was gradually diminishing; he went alone to see the counselor a few times, but he still didn't want his anger treated as a problem to be solved. By fiercely resisting all our efforts to make him talk, he made it clear that he wanted the freedom to deal with things as he chose. At $120 an hour and with no insurance to cover it, neither Janice nor I was inclined to push the issue. He only seemed angry when we did prod him to talk about his anger, so we took the path of least resistance. Still today he keeps his interior life hidden from me and, I'd guess, from most people, although he has no inhibitions about acting out his feelings. Seeing him be frustrated or upset or angry and not being able to get him to tell me why, I suddenly understand what life must be like for many women whose husbands are afflicted with this same difficulty. I hope he doesn't shut out his future wife this way, but I suspect he will.

When he wasn't stormy, we had good times. We tossed the old pill out in the yard, just like a cartoon Dad and Son; we had softball gloves and played catch, and I had him added to the roster of our coed media-league softball team; we had a spell of tennis, we went bowling and I helped him practice soccer. He has a lot of natural talent and grace; then, he was small for his age but was very quick and wiry, with sharp reflexes and the sort of courage that, as a goalie on his soccer team, made him frequently make kamikaze dives to stop shots from being scored against him. He didn't mind getting hurt. (Instead, he seemed to welcome it sometimes, and that worried me.) No matter what we played, he was better at it, really, and only my size and experience made me able to keep up with him.

As a kid, I was almost always among the last chosen or my name was lumped in a herd in a negotiation ("Okay, you take everybody from Jimmy on down and I'll take . . ."). I wasn't bookish, though; I was strong and healthy and enjoyed playing, but I had little talent, and I'd worn glasses since I was in the second grade. In the ninth grade, I had forced myself to endure a season of football just to get a letter to wear on my jacket, but after that I faced the truth that I wasn't a jock.

Now, suddenly, participating in all these sports with Keith, I felt unprepared, as if I had been, out of the blue, assigned the job of coaching him. I felt like an imposter and wondered if he wouldn't have been a lot better off with an ex-jock as a father, the way he took to these things so naturally. I forgot that these are, really, a boy's pursuits. Keith read the sports section of the newspaper; when we went to the barbershop, he'd peruse *Sports Illustrated,* then he and my barber would trade NFL trivia notes. Keith was a much better student of sports than I, and our barber no doubt thought Keith was more a man. I had a subscription to *Sports Illustrated* sent to his house for the next year or so. And has he become a star athlete? In his teens, his most vigorous exercise is brushing his teeth after smoking a Marlboro. But—tortoise and the hare—I'm still jogging.

I longed to be a Norman Rockwell father, and that's why we took up the cudgels and wickets so fast and furiously. Fishing was far too boring to even pretend an interest in; hunting was too expensive, seasonal and dangerous. Beyond my wanting him to feel normal and beyond my wanting to feel that myself, there was the simple matter of our doing something—anything—together. Each pitch caught and tossed back was a stitch in the fabric that enfolded us; even if years from then we both confessed we really had no zest for tennis and that we were only playing because we thought the other wanted it, then at least our mutual pretense would have constituted mutual acts of selflessness, and blessed be the tie that binds.

Sometimes I would blissfully wrap myself in thoughts about these domestic activities even as I was doing them, so that I could remind myself that my life had the semblance of normality. But it had the semblance, not the essence, and that was the catch. No matter how hard we might try, the four of us were not a family, and sometimes desperately engaging in "family" activities only served to nail that point down more tightly. We were two groups, even when we were together, one composed of me and the kids, the other of me and Marcia. When we were in the apartment together, I could sense these two constituencies pulling at me from opposite poles, vying for the greater claim to my attention and affection, setting up no-win dilemmas: the lady or the tigers.

And were *they* at odds?

The first time Keith and Nicole met Marcia, she and I were living apart from our spouses and from one another. She drove an old but very serviceable Chevy that she kept immaculate. No sooner were my children in it than they tore several pieces of notebook paper into confetti, which they then scattered like snowflakes all over the back seat. The next time I got them togther, it was at Marcia's apartment. After we had eaten, we all sat on her bed in the dark to tell ghost stories, but they kept pelting us with Corn Nuts. When they saw me hugging her, they would cackle, race around us, leap onto my back or grab me around the legs from behind. Or they would go into another room and begin screaming and fighting.

Later, after we were both divorced and had moved into an apartment together, we kept a spare bedroom for their weekend visits. The elderly landlady lived downstairs, and while she approved of our having my children visit, she did live alone, quietly, and we didn't want to disturb her. Once, soon after we had moved into the apartment, the kids came over for supper during the week, and later that night I had to leave to attend a meeting. This was Marcia's first time in charge of them; prior to this, she had been something like an aunt or older sister—she had shied away from being parental—and no sooner was I out the front door than both kids galloped wildly about the house, yelling. Then Nicole lay prone on the floor, beat on it with her fists and feet and screamed, "Can you hear me down there?" Horrified, Marcia had to scream back at her to stop.

When they visited, they would literally hang on me, fighting with each other for my attention. Even if they were engaged quite comfortably in watching TV or reading, their radar would inform them that Marcia and I had wound up together in a room somewhere, and they would come running to separate us by asking me to do something. If we were in our bedroom with the door open, they would run in and jump on the bed; if the door was closed, they would knock on it every minute or so with some trumped-up request.

Fascinated, Nicole would browse through Marcia's cosmetics and the knickknacks on her dresser, sometimes using them without permission, misplacing them or asking if she could have them. When we declared our bedroom off-limits, that only intensified their desire to wedge themselves between us. Although she had helped to raise her half-sister, Marcia was unaccustomed to children and she was continually upset at how I couldn't seem to control them, how when she complained about them, all I did was to rationalize their behavior.

At the dinner table, they pinched, kicked, slapped and

cursed each other, disrupting the meal and getting a rise out of me, so that for months, it seemed, every meal was aborted by my shouting and someone being sent away from the table. Marcia began to dread sitting down to eat in her own house; it made her stomach hurt, she said. I didn't want her to eat apart from us for fear someone would notice that we weren't a happy family of four.

"Where do you go?" she asked one Sunday night after we had had a particularly exhausting weekend. "I'd like to be able to get away like that."

"What do you mean?"

"I mean when they're here you just withdraw. You just get this glaze over your eyes and walk around like a zombie. I wish I could do it."

"I didn't know I did."

"If you were me trying to contact you, you would. I don't like having my weekends taken up by your kids, but I'm willing to do it for you, so long as we're in this together. But when you close yourself off, it doesn't make them go away for me. I'm still here cooking and cleaning up their messes and worrying about what they're going to get into. My reward ought to be at least that I feel I'm with you."

Where did I go? To the secret room in the attic of my brain. I was an only child until age five; I spent many pleasurable days there, and as an adult it was still very satisfying to sneak up those narrow stairs whenever there was confict on the floors below. Up there I didn't have to face the fear that Marcia and my children wouldn't (didn't) really care for one another, wouldn't (didn't) really accept one another, that they would demand that I choose between them. I simply didn't want to be present if that happened, so it seemed wise to be deaf and blind and to pretend that four people sitting to dinner could be an instant family because I wanted them to be.

Because what I desired was this—to have the family I had before, only slightly remodeled, with a new kitchen, as it were, a replacement of the Maternal Parental Unit with a New, Improved one. To foster the illusion that I had successfully performed this trick, now and then I engineered an occasion like the following party, which my diary notes as "backyard bbq with friends and kids and friends' kids."

I wanted to have friends from my old life over so that they wouldn't think I had divorced them, too, and also to give them a chance to assure me that I was still held in esteem. Janice and I had agreed on joint custody of our friends, but the friends who normally surround a separating couple are always made uneasy regardless of the civility of the divorce.

My idea was that this would be a "family" affair. There'd be four other couples, two of them with children of their own. We'd sit outside in lawn chairs around the old gas grill, drink some beer, chat and talk, supervise our children while they caught fireflies in jars and played hide-and-seek in the waning twilight. *Here's to good friends, the night is kind of special . . .*

My idea was to perpetuate the illusion that I hadn't left anything behind when I divorced, or, rather, that I hadn't *lost* anything I hadn't wanted to lose. I wanted to feel like any other suburban father at home. I didn't know this then. I was only struck by the impulse to give a party on a Saturday night when the kids were staying over.

Marcia balked. She had been ill with a bronchial infection for days, and, looking ahead to the weekend, she didn't have much enthusiasm for giving a party for my old friends and their children.

"Look, it won't be any trouble for you," I promised. "I'll take care of everything."

It would be just a simple, slapped-together meal, I assured her, just stuff off the grill. I'd take care of the meat, I'd make some potato salad, etc.

I browbeat her into agreeing. As the weekend approached, my menu became more elaborate, and Marcia observed with alarm as I made extra trips to the gourmet food store for exotica, wine and hard liquor—"I thought you said just beer and cokes!"—and before she knew it, I was marinating chicken and brisket and sausage and had the fixings for cole slaw, potato salad, pinto beans, as well as chips and dips, several kinds of colas and an assortment of foreign and domestic beers.

She was a little bewildered. Obviously, something was afoot, and she felt obligated to help prepare the food, to make lists for items. Then she began to sense that she was going to be on display.

"Would Janice make a cake?" she asked.

"Huh? Why do you want to know?"

"I just do."

"No." Janice had been known to let people sit in her living room for an hour without offering them anything to drink—that was my job in our marriage, but Marcia didn't know that.

"Good," she said. "Then I'll make one."

"Great!" I said.

She looked askance at my enthusiasm. Oh, my orchestration was going well. I had slyly escalated the party until it was almost large enough to satisfy my desire to be a good host and to prove that, at last, I had a good hostess beside me; I had manipulated Marcia into assuming part of the responsibility for this *festive celebration of my new family,* even though she had been sick and didn't want to spend the weekend entertaining Janice's friends.

To convince myself that I had managed to reconstruct

my family, I needed Marcia to play the New, Improved Maternal Parental Unit in it. If Marcia got into her part, then she'd get a sense of being in the family, of being the sated, pleasantly inebriated suburban adult content and relaxed because the kids are playing within earshot and the sky above the yard is atwinkle with stars and winking fireflies.

I did prepare most of the food, and at the party, after I fired up the grill and placed myself in manly supervision over the meat, I popped the tabs off the beers and tended to people's drinks. But then I seemed to steer clear of what was suddenly to my mind classified as woman's work. When Marcia saw that the food was not being brought out, that the tables outside were not being set, that the colas and tea and ice and silverware and plates were not being conveyed from inside to outside, she naturally didn't want anybody to think she had gone on strike, even though I had promised to do everything, so she set to work.

I had suddenly labeled this woman's work because I started wondering what picture my friends would have of my new family if my new mate was even *less* willing than my old one (who had been moderately unwilling) to play hostess. Thanks to Marcia's falling into my trap, the meal went smoothly. For me. She went up and down the back stairs a couple of dozen times to retrieve things people needed while I accepted compliments on the food and made great progress on a twelve-pack of Moosehead. It seemed to me that we were having a great party there in the backyard. My friends were gathered around me in my lawn chairs, chatting merrily, while my New, Improved mate flitted about taking care of the mundane details such as carrying the dirty plates upstairs and bringing down clean ones to serve the cake on and making certain that some kid who spilled his Nehi received another to spill later.

This left me free to entertain my guests by sharing with them my expansive personality and bountiful charm.

And so while we carried on about matters big and little, airing our opinions, sharing our jokes, the children would appear and momentarily attach themselves to the perimeter of our circle to complain that someone wasn't sharing a toy or that a hot dog had dropped in the dirt. I grew cozy and warm in my cocoon, remembering church or company picnics from my childhood when we kids would swarm about playing tag or chase while overhead was the steady, comforting drone of adult conversation.

Ah, I thought. I'm giving Marcia and my children a taste of old Norman Rockwell *Post*-cover life everybody thought had vanished from America. O blissful dullness! O bounteous bourgeoisieness! Heavenly domestic serenity! I could have drunk a toast: "To good friends, to Easter egg hunts with knee-high toddlers in pink dresses, to K mart and Pizza Hut, to your dollar Disney-movie houses! And to the fountain and ferns in our lovely shopping malls!"

Just at the moment when I might have been lifting my bottle to utter such a toast, Marcia was returning up the back stairs with an armful of dirty dishes and the remainder of the cake, with some stranger's child clinging to her leg and bawling because her chubby little fingers had been separated from the icing on the cake when Marcia had lifted it from the table.

In the kitchen, she found the floor slick and sticky with spilled cola—she who never walks out of a kitchen after a meal before completely and thoroughly cleaning it. The counters were filled with empty bottles, dirty plates, the sink full of dirty silverware, ice bags torn open. In the breakfast room, she saw that a child had spilled Coke on the new carpet. A pottery bowl was missing from its usual place on the sideboard. Since she'd grown up as an army brat and moved more frequently than she wanted, she had a stronger than usual need for neatness, tidiness and order in her home. She knew the precise placement of every object; on entering a room, her eyes instantly scanned the contents and the data was fed into her interior computer, so that within milliseconds she could tell you that a book on the coffee table has been moved an inch since the last time she was present.

She heard the children running and screaming somewhere in the house, but she couldn't see them. There were my two ten-year-olds, a girl a little older, and two younger boys. As she passed through the dining room, one of them poked a head around a corner, spotted her, squealed and screamed to the others and vanished. As Marcia made her way into the living room, she heard their thundering footfalls and giggles as they disappeared into a bedroom off the living room.

Quickly, she moved to the bedroom my children used on their visits, opened the door, found still another mess— they had eaten in the room despite orders not to, just as they had ignored her request that they play outside—but, once again, there were giggles and footfalls as they raced to elude her. She saw them darting out of our bedroom. When she went into it, she noticed that nothing was missing nor had anything been spilled—but things on her dresser had been handled, moved about slightly, *as if just to let her know they could get away with it.*

Out in the hallway, she walked to the large closet at the end, hearing a rustling and bumping behind the door, and when she opened it, the small pack of them, led by my cackling twins, burst out and around her and ran away, clambering down the rear stairs and outside, where I was by now finishing my toast to the joy of solid family life.

The closet looked like a bargain basement. Strewn across

the floor were Marcia's sweaters and slacks, wool scarves and gloves, all winter clothes that had been carefully put away in boxes a few months earlier.

Holding back her tears, she walked into the dark study then sat down to cry. She wondered if when she showed me this damage, I would try to minimize the significance of it by saying these kids were just being energetic, high-spirited. Would I try to deny that the whole herd was obviously being led by my children and that there was something particularly personal in this attack? That she was the specific target?

Other things came to her mind now, too. She had a stressful job as a reporter and needed her weekends to unwind, but she had been sacrificing them so that I could stay in touch with my children. But since she was not even their stepmother, she had no say in how they were disciplined. She wasn't getting to spend any good time with the man for whom she had divorced her first husband, a promising young executive.

What had she gotten herself into?

There had been this charming older man, an author no less, a colleague, toward whom she had had a romantic and sexual attraction. She had been a big reader as a kid, and becoming the lover of an older author was in a way the consummate expression of her girlish longings. Now that the mist had dissipated, she found herself playing maid and cook and handmaiden to two brats who were jealous of the time she spent with their father and angry at her for taking him away from them. Out in her backyard were several adults a good decade older than she who were no doubt comparing her unfavorably with the ex-wife; while she wanted to be accepted, she didn't want to lose ten years of her life by skipping ahead. And that's what it made her feel—*he* might be feeling more youthful by having taken up with a woman fourteen years his junior, but he seemed to expect her to look, act, think and talk forty-two and not twenty-eight. God knows she was close enough to being thirty, and she certainly didn't want to find herself being thirty going on forty-five.

Then there was how their plans always had to follow Janice's. They couldn't think about going away for a weekend without first making sure she would be free to stay with the kids; they couldn't plan a vacation without first checking to make certain Janice was not already planning to be gone.

Their outings at restaurants were a torment. Sitting at a table as a foursome, clearly only barely old enough to be the children's mother, she felt branded, stared at. She felt as if she were a substitute for Janice, sitting inside the outlines of *her* ghost. The feeling of being outside, of not belonging, was old and familiar but never quite comfortable—it brought back too many unpleasant memories of moving to a new place and coming up to kids on the block who had been friends with each other since nursery school. She was an intruder, and she had always been forced to adapt to someone else's ready-made situation.

Little relief lay ahead. He was profoundly attached to them, and she appreciated that—her father had divorced her mother when she was five and had made only lame attempts to stay in touch—but it meant she would be living with his children for another ten years, at least. Raising them took most of his extra energy and income and attention, so it wasn't likely that he was going to want any more children. So long as she stayed with him, she would likely be childless, though she'd have to coexist with his children. She'd have to help raise someone else's teenagers without being allowed the joy of having had her own infant, toddler, preschooler. She'd have to help raise children who resented her.

And didn't respect him. The way he let them run over him anguished her—it made her mad at them for not understanding what a good man he was, and it made her furious at him for not sticking up for himself. They cursed him, deliberately disobeyed his orders, manipulated him, by the very large handle of his guilt. He had a forceful personality, otherwise; it had been his strut, his quiet, graceful show of confidence, that had originally caught her eye.

But now with his children he seemed wishy-washy, beaten. His son would goad him by bad behavior into making an ultimatum—"You'll clean up that mess you made or else you won't be leaving your room tonight!"—but then his son would neither clean up his room nor stay in it. So to save face, his father would officially rescind the terms of the punishment—allowing him to clean half the mess—to fit what the son was willing to do. At the very time in their lives when they needed his strength, it had dissipated. It made her angry with him because it made him unattractive.

The kids understood what was happening. Recently they all had gone bowling. Keith had not done as well as Nicole during the first line, so he got mad and refused to play another. He sat on the bench scowling, blaming his low score on preposterous causes such as the alley, the ball, having to follow Nicole. He jeered at her and tried to rattle her as they struggled to continue without him. He was being such an obnoxious brat that she wanted to strangle him, but all the Great Love of Her Life could do was whine that his behavior wasn't appropriate. His son said petulantly, "Give me some quarters. I want to play video games while you bowl." And he got them.

She watched Nicole watch this, saw her grow pensive as she had been many times lately when father and son were fighting. It worried her sometimes that Nicole was left out simply because she was quieter, that his son was so fiercely aggressive in capturing his father's attention. When Keith came to visit alone, he seemed calmer, quieter, better able to occupy himself, but when he came with Nicole, it aroused this ferocious need to win their father's affection. Keith was astonishingly greedy for it and couldn't seem to allow Nicole even the most measly scrap.

Coming out of the bowling alley, Keith said, "Gimme a piggy-back ride!"

And he got it.

Nicole was hanging back, looking sad. When they had gotten home, she had watched Nicole go off by herself into the living room, looking glum. She followed her and said, "I think I know what you're feeling. You're upset because of Keith and how he always gets what he wants because he's so noisy about it." Nicole nodded.

Marcia went back into her bedroom and retrieved some eye-shadow Nicole had been asking for, then took it back into the living room.

"Here," she said, handing it to her, "I know you've been wanting this."

"You don't have to give me something just because I'm acting bad," she said, surprised.

Marcia told her she had only meant to cheer her up with the gift. From then on she and Nicole had gotten along much better. Unlike Keith, Nicole would talk to her as if she were simply another person. They went shopping together a couple of times, and Marcia had taken her to a ballet, and these pleasant times alone with her had brought back the half-forgotten pleasures of being an older sister. Alone with her, Nicole gave in to her natural inclination to like people, but when she was with her father and Keith, she was compelled to ally herself with her absent mother and her brother against the Other Woman.

Keith, on the other hand, frequently acted as if she were invisible. If he came into a room where she was alone, he'd often find some pretext to leave it, and if someone else were there, he would usually talk to the third party. At the table, he hardly ever glanced her way. The way neither could ask something of her without posing the question through their father drove Marcia to distraction.

Sometimes she thought everything would be better if they were married. Then she would be able to speak as a wife and not merely as a live-in whom they might secretly be thinking they could outlast. And she could have at least an equal claim to him, too. As it stood now, she performed all the duties and chores of a wife and mother without the status of either; she suffered the stigma of stepmotherhood without the rights. He was their legal and biological father whose blood they shared, and this formed some holy circle that no mere cohabiting girlfriend could ever hope to break to gain entrance.

Not long after that party, I made another entry in my diary: "Marcia and I quarrel about getting married."

Usually when she raised the question, I got scared. She and I had a much more powerful union than my marriage had ever been, and I harbored an irrational suspicion that getting married might hex it. Having wrecked one marriage had destroyed my confidence in the future of any relationship no matter how sound it might seem at the time; now I knew just how fickle the human heart (my own) could be, and I was old enough to know that the future had a nasty way of delivering to your doorstep precisely what you might have presumed to be inconceivable.

*145*

There lurked another, equally irrational, reason for holding back. I had very carefully and judiciously apportioned myself out between Marcia and my children, holding my breath up there on that tightrope, feeling the weight of their mutually exclusive allegiance tugging on one side or another. I had managed to maintain an equilibrium; I tried to convey to Marcia that divorcing Janice had constituted a commitment to her; I tried to convey to Keith and Nicole that I was still committed to them.

So I worried that getting married might send the kids a signal that Marcia had "won." I worried that they could see it as a sign of a diminishing love for them, perhaps even a harbinger of outright abandonment. I worried that it would make them feel they had lost me for good.

When I balked, it hurt Marcia's pride. She wanted me to be the one who wanted marriage; she wanted to be the one who had to be coaxed into it—having the converse violated her fondest storybook notions about love and marriage. She accused me of lacking confidence in our relationship, of losing interest in her.

But she didn't care to be a two-time loser, either. All I had to do to make *her* reluctance blossom was to sprinkle hope on it. When I warmed to a marriage and quit raising objections, suddenly she had to face the real possibility of it. Then, my agreement was not just a sign of my love— all at once it was a prelude to an act that only required a commitment from her. When she drew up a list of assets and liabilities relating to marriage, about the only asset was me; the other side of the ledger had forbidding entries that included raising my children and not having her own, being restricted to where the children were living and curbing career possibilities that might arise elsewhere, and spending several years in penury with me—I had no savings or retirement funds; my expenditures on my children made it difficult to take a vacation with her unless she bought it for me. My visible assets were a car and a few pieces of furniture. My child support would officially end when they turned eighteen, but then they would be entering college. Barring some windfall, it wasn't likely that we could ever own a house together. I kept insisting that some day I would make money as a writer, but in the four years she had known me my income from that source had amounted to about enough to make a down payment for the house I lost to Janice in the settlement and to pay for a divorce lawyer. I had a teaching job from year to year, a part-time job at that, while I kept reinvesting my spare time and energy in projects that had no assurance of success. I could hear her fuming: Where did I get off saying no when she tried to pressure me into marrying her? Beside her sacrifices in such a marrriage, what in the world were mine? She could tell me precisely what she would be giving up, and what could I match it with?

*March 28, Friday. David, Amy, Keith, Nicole here for birthday party. Marcia furious over having privacy invaded.*

Holidays and birthdays were difficult because nobody knew the rules. Without any traditions, every occasion had to be negotiated. Would they have Thanksgiving dinner at Janice's house or mine? Their Christmases were spent pursuing an itinerary as carefully wrought as that of a diplomatic visit. If they awakened at their home on Christmas morning, then we would expect Janice to bring them to us after they had opened presents there so that we could have them for lunch (or dinner) and have our Christmas. Christmas without them would have been bleak compared to those I enjoyed when they were preschoolers, but watching them travel from house to house merely to appease my need to have them present, I felt sorry for them. Having them for a few hours or even overnight didn't quite do the trick because they were, after all, only visitors, and their *real* tree and their *real* Christmas was across town. They were like Rent-a-Kids, props for a private Christmas pageant.

I was worse about using them as props on Father's day and on my birthday. I don't know when I got the notion of myself as a patriarch, but I saw my birthdays this way— in an olive grove in Sicily, there's a very long table set with white cloths, with hordes of nicely dressed children and adults all paying homage to the elderly *don* who's drooling on his bib at the head of the table. A toast to Don Carlos! May he live forever!

Janice had always observed my birthday in a very low-key way, but Marcia, who knew more about me, knew that the most important aspect of my birthday was the opportunity to pretend to be a normal father. She went out of her way to cook something special, to make a cake, to arrange privately for Nicole and Keith to be present on the appointed day and to remind them to make or buy a present for me. The kids weren't at all reluctant to observe my birthday, and seeing their pleasure in giving me something gave me pleasure.

On the evening noted by the diary entry, Marcia had called a couple we knew and asked them to come to dinner with us and the kids. We adults sat around sipping wine and chatting for awhile, then Marcia fed us lasagne and banana pudding (a favorite of mine). I opened the kids' cards and gifts, then opened the card from Marcia.

"Don't read it out loud," she warned.

It was a Paper Moon card with a scene of a guy and a girl lying in the front seat of a '57 Chevy. The viewer's perspective is from the rear seat, and all we see is the couple's arms extended straight above the back of the seat. His senior's ring is twinkling in the light, and she seems to be reaching for it.

"What's it say, Dad?" Nicole asked, suddenly curious.

Inside, Marcia had written a graphic description of the couple's activity, using "you" and "me" in place of "he" and "she."

"It's R-rated," I joked. "You'll have to wait until you're seventeen."

After all the gifts had been opened, I took the card back to our bedroom and set it on top of our dresser to keep it from being read not only by the kids but also by our adult guests.

The adults retired to the living room to continue talking and drinking, while Keith and Nicole went into their room to watch TV. Shortly after, Nicole came to the door, grinned and said, "David, come here! We want to show you something!"

Our friend David got up and left the room. After a minute or so, he came back, holding the R-rated card. He was grinning, but he looked a little sheepish. He said, "Hey, Marcia, this is pretty hot stuff."

Nicole had gone into our bedroom obviously to find the card, and she had taken it to her room for Keith to read. Then they had shown it to David. He handed me the card, and I returned it to the bedroom, though this time (too late!) I put it in a drawer of my dresser. As I passed back by the door to the kids' room, I stuck my head in.

"Hey, that wasn't a very nice thing to do, Nicole," I said.

"Okay," she said, but then she giggled.

Frowning, I left and returned to the living room. David

and Amy were saying good night, having sensed the tension in the air. Marcia's chin was quivering minutely, and she was struggling to keep from breaking into tears.

She went into our bedroom and finally she cried. At first I tried to console her by minimizing the importance of what had happened.

"You really didn't say anything very racy on that card," I said. "Nobody's going to be shocked by it."

"Do you really think that's the point?"

I played dumb and tried to get her to tell me what the point was, but she merely lay with her face in her hands, her shoulders shaking. I knew what the point was: Nicole had not just wanted to know what was written on the card; she had wanted to pass it around and show it even to David before we discovered that it had been read. Her aim had been to achieve the maximum audience so that Marcia's embarrassment would be greater. Had she merely wanted to read the card, she could have sneaked a look and kept mum about it.

"I can understand why you're angry," I said finally.

"I'm not just angry. I'm depressed," she said. "This isn't working out."

With a huge trembling sigh, she began to talk about how it was clear that I was never going to be able to stand up to my kids even when one had deliberately insulted or humiliated her. Here she paid half the rent, and she didn't even have a room to call her own in her own house—my children had a room, but she herself didn't. The bedroom also belonged to me, and I had a study to myself. And despite all the times we had told them not to go into our room without permission, Nicole had completely violated Marcia's privacy.

And all I ever did about it was apologize for them.

"I'm sorry," I said.

"It's not enough."

"What do you want me to do?"

"There's nothing you can do," she said grimly. She rolled over and refused to talk any more.

I tried to decide if she meant that she didn't want to figure something out for me to do, if she felt it was my job to do that, or if she had truly reached the point where no redress was possible.

Maybe she meant that it wasn't within my power because I was a spineless wimp. Maybe she was saying I had to act in keeping with my character.

The longer I sat there feeling as if I had lost her out of my weakness, the angrier I got at Nicole.

I got up and went into their bedroom where I gave her a tongue lashing such as I had not done in a long while. I demanded that they both apologize to Marcia. Nicole was humbled by my indignation and fury, and she went into the hallway and stood abashed at the threshold of our bedroom. Keith followed suit, but his attitude stank—*I'm doing this because someone's making me.* They had both been such horrible little jerks on my birthday that I slammed the door in their faces and lay down beside Marcia. I tried to console her.

After about three minutes or so, either Keith or Nicole knocked on the door.

"Go away!" I screamed. A tremendous rush of liberation swept through me—I was so angry I no longer felt guilty, so angry I could order them to go away without any regrets, so angry that I didn't care what they did or what happened to them. For a moment, I had regained my rightful place as the responsible adult whose authority must be both respected and obeyed. Suddenly, Marcia and I had both taken sufficient abuse to pay for our sins, and now I was howling that the punishment far outstripped the crimes.

To Marcia, it was a gratifying sign of my loyalty—it was the first time I had ever stuck up for her. But in the year and a half since I had left home, it was the first time I had stuck up for myself, too, and I realized I had grown too comfortable sitting in the ashes.

They tiptoed about the rest of the evening, a little awestruck. I was pleased with myself. It was the best birthday gift they could have given me, returning to me my truest, best sense of fatherhood.

But then I had no idea of how prophetic my command for them to "Go away!" would be.

# EIGHT

## Long Distance

As 1982 rolled along, the rhythms of everyday life lulled me into a cozy sleep-walk. It seemed possible to be happy without causing unhappiness, or at least the sadness my divorce had caused my children had finite limits. They had gone through the worst, I thought. After almost three years, our situation seemed stable. Although there were spats, flare-ups and skirmishes, generally Keith and Nicole seemed to have accepted my new life, and I felt I had done a good job of bringing them into it.

So Marcia and I made plans to be married; we would include my children in the ceremony, and they were invited to discuss the music, the cake, the place and time with us.

But we were no sooner married in late October, with them at our sides, than Janice announced that she was taking a new job in a city three hundred miles away, on the Gulf Coast. She and the kids would be moving within a month.

This news struck like a heretofore suspended judgment on my life, the way, when I was a cild, I imagined that a transgression had gone unnoticed merely because the condemnation had not yet been declared by my parents who'd just been waiting for the right time. *Things had been going too well, I was too happy,* I thought. *I forgot I would have to pay for it.* If they moved I couldn't cruise over on a moment's notice or plan a pizza dinner for a Wednesday night, the sole purpose of which was hugging them when they came out their front door. Now no matter what terrible thing happened to them, I wouldn't be available to help.

How could they live without me? How could I live without them? I panicked. I didn't have room to keep them both, but I invited Keith to live with me because he had asked earlier. He turned me down, whether from resentment or loyalty to his sister and his mother, I don't know.

For three weeks prior to their moving, they stayed in our apartment while Janice looked for a house in their new city. They had just started junior high, and as the days went by I grew jealous because they wanted to spend time saying good-bye to their friends. I wanted to give them such a booster shot of myself that they'd never be able to get me out of their system. A desperate urgency set in as I shuttled them to school, to their friends' houses, to the skating rink, to the mall, as I bought last-minute school supplies and doled out lunch money and allowances—I kept wanting to say, "See how much you need me?" The urge was irrational and childish—they were not responsible for this separation and had no control over it. And here, I stumbled onto a paradox of being a parent: It required me to be more adult than does any other activity I engage in but it seemed to make me more subjective and temperamental; that is, it required my best but encouraged my worst.

The Sunday before their departure on Tuesday, November 16, I labored over dinner so that when we sat to eat,

154

they'd be able to recall how life at my house seemed conventional. In turn, in the future they would experience this the way other, normal kids had. My near obsession with the conventional stemmed from a desire for my children to be able to move about comfortably in the world without having their difference broadcast unless they chose to have it known; it came from a desire to minimize their future trouble by allowing them to pretend that some of their life had been Cleaveresque. At least they could feel they had been introduced to Cleaveresque rituals the way they were introduced to Christianity by attending church on Easter and Christmas. They would be able to *pass* as kids with a conventional background.

They balked at coming to the table, however. They wanted to eat in their room and watch TV. "Mom never makes us eat at the table," Nicole said. Rather than explain my desire to teach them to pass as Cleaver kids, I whined that I had slaved in the kitchen for hours—well, the pot roast had been cooking that long, anyway—so that we could enjoy a Sunday family dinner.

Keith retorted, "This isn't our family."

That comment stung me for two more days, until Tuesday, when they left, and the bitter truth of it made my saying good-bye especially difficult, since the parting seemed one-sided. Why should they be upset at leaving me? They weren't leaving their family. I helped them pack, then hugged them hard when Janice came to get them. "I'll see you real soon," I kept saying, since we had already made plans to see them during Thanksgiving a couple of weeks away. And then Christmas would soon follow, and they'd come for a visit then. "I'll see you real soon," I said. "I'll see you real soon."

I signed up for Sprint. When they were settled, I called them nightly. I kept thinking, *It won't be so bad*—but it was. I was tormented by not knowing how their rooms were decorated, what the house looked like—they said it was situated about a mile back from the beach and was "on stilts." I didn't know anything about their school; their teachers had no faces. Their teachers didn't know me, either, and so my children were fatherless to them. If some kid said to them, "What's your dad do?" they'd say he was a professor somewhere else and they didn't live with him, and that kid—or it might be an adult—would picture my children as orphans or crippled kids missing something essential.

They rode a school bus, they said. I coaxed from Nicole a yard-by-yard description of the route to school, picturing how the bus passed over a bridge (a causeway?), with the water below "kind of glittery, you know, when it's early and the sun is shining on it," she said.

I thought of Chappaquiddick. Frolicking in the surf, they were swept out to sea by riptides, undertow. Sharks cleaved their limbs from their bodies; blue jellyfish draped high-voltage tentacles across my children's fair, thin skin. Alone in the house after school, they singed their palms on the stove burners and electrocuted themselves by turning on their hair dryers while standing in the tub.

Once I learned that Keith had stayed home from school alone for two days, sick. At his age when I was sick, my mother checked on me every hour, plumped my pillow, refilled a water glass or brought me a 7-Up, laid her warm palm over my brow; she would coo and cluck and act as if I had every right in the world to feel sorry for myself. Home from work, my dad would cheer me up with a joke.

"I'm sorry to hear you were sick," I told Keith over the phone, then, as if it were his fault I hadn't known, I added, "You should have called me and told me!"

"I'm fine."

He was always "fine." Nicole was always "fine," too, even though, unknown to me, a great dark pterodactyl of depression was making a slow bank before gliding in to land on her ribcage.

These telephone interrogations were fruitless.

"What did you do in school today?"

"Nothing."

"Who are your friends?"

"Just some kids."

"Where do these kids live?"

"Aw, you know, everywhere."

"What do you all do when you get together?"

"Just stuff."

Getting information from adolescents is hard for many live-in parents too, I realized, but since I didn't know how my children's friends dressed, spoke or acted, my imagination could either lull me into serenity or knock on my door at midnight just as I was drifting off to sleep to inform me that a traffic accident involving several stoned teenagers had "claimed the life" of my children.

The phone was a crucial link. Sometimes I worked to hear in their voices all the minute aspects of their lives, the way I replay small night sounds in my inner ear to judge them malign or benign; while we talked, I would ask them where they were sitting, what they had eaten that day, what they were wearing. They now had garments I had never seen. They had no interest in the details of their own lives and couldn't believe that such trivia was of importance to me. I couldn't get enough information about them to set my mind at ease. To be satisfied, I needed an exact and comprehensive conception of what every minute of their lives was like, and I had to depend on their reluctant, inarticulate descriptions to construct it; it was like trying to build a house with my bare hands. I longed to be a single fiber-optic strand so I could zip down the line and come crawling out a hole in the mouthpiece of their phone. Never had the Ma Bell slogan "Reach Out and Touch Someone" seemed such an outrageous lie.

To them, these interrogations were a rip-roaring bore. Invariably when I called they were about to watch CHiPS, to eat, to get a call from a friend or to get out of the shower, and answering Uncle Dad's survey was as appealing as having a chat with a magazine subscription peddler.

I was far on the periphery of their lives. If there had been trouble at school I wouldn't know about it, unless, say, Nicole mentioned that Keith had been beaten up by a black gang *last week* or how he had called his band director an "asshole," which Keith would instantly deny, calling Nicole a troublemaker and a liar and leaving me helpless to sort out the facts, let alone impose discipline. My father would have whipped me for calling a teacher an ugly name to his face. But then my father had not divorced my mother.

Many times when I talked to Keith and Nicole, I felt I was hearing the kind of bland and superficial phrases about their lives such as I was accustomed to giving to my own distant grandparents over the telephone when I was a child, and this perspective on how little I counted would leave me sad and angry, especially when it was obvious that they didn't really want to talk. When I complained, Marcia said, "You're not letting them have any choice about when to talk to you. Ease up and give them a chance to call you."

Once I waited for days, feeling as bruised, anxious and fretful as an adolescent girl yearning for the phone to ring. Finally, convinced that if I walked out of their lives altogether they would never miss me, I broke down and called them. If they were aware of any hiatus in our calls, they didn't mention it. Bundled cozily in self-pity, it seemed to me that I wanted to be their father more than they wanted me to be. And even then, at the very moment of thinking this, I hadn't lost sight of how I had chosen to leave them.

I begged them to call me. "Sure, Dad, we will," they said. "When?" I'd say. "Tomorrow." Then, when tomorrow came and I'd get no call, I'd get too antsy to wait any longer; I'd pick up the phone and whine, "Why didn't you call me?" "Golly," one or the other would say. "I was going to."

Trying to be a father by long distance, I was anxious and aggrieved anew. That spring, I had frequent colds and viruses; I developed high blood pressure and muscle spasms, and my weight suddenly ballooned to twenty pounds over normal. At the time I chalked all these changes up to aging, but now it seems clear that they were symptoms of stress.

Gradually I learned telephone technique. I'd check the TV schedule to avoid pulling them away from their favorite shows, though these appeared to be almost anything on prime time. I endured episodes of *The A-Team* so that I could discuss them (is this not the ultimate in parental sacrifice?), even though the pervasive imagery there— burning autos leaping like trained dogs through burning hoops—diabolically dramatized the very nightmares I was having about my kids.

Instead of grilling them with the same questions, I would talk about my day or my work or my car or my wife or my friends, as if they had asked and as if they cared— which, surprisingly, they sometimes did. One guy I knew told me he talked with his kids about his pets and their pets, and this worked with Nicole. Sometimes I would ask about movies they had seen. This worked especially well with Keith, because every twelve-year-old boy has a gene that compels him to describe every frame of a movie he sees. I would let the content of his speech wash over me; I would listen instead to his inflection, his diction, the structure of his sentences and to his mood. My ear was a stethoscope pressed to his voice, listening for his heartbeat.

These telephone tricks didn't really improve the quality of the information I got, but they did keep my frustration at a minimum and let me think that at least my calls were letting my children know I still loved them, still missed them, still thought about them.

My anxiety would vanish only when they were present, before my eyes and ears, during their monthly weekend visits. Like the phone calls, these visits came to have an inevitable emotional cycle as chartable as menses.

A visit: High anticipation makes me step lightly, whistling, as I stride down the halls of the airport where I eagerly await their flight. I've been thinking about greeting them for days, and I've been busy thinking about where we can all go together tomorrow. It's Friday evening and they'll only be here until Sunday afternoon when I have to put them on a flight back home. So we have tonight, tomorrow, tomorrow night and Sunday morning. I can think of a million things to do, but they are twelve now and many of these things they're simply not interested in. They're much too blasé for museums and zoos; board games are boring; movies are still all right so long as they are rated R and they'll still tolerate flea markets. Basically, I would like just to sit and stare at them, adore them, study their hands and faces and the nape of their necks, but they won't put up with that.

My plans have come to this: I've made a batch of spaghetti that's on the stove, so we can unpack, eat, then hang around my apartment for tonight. Maybe I can get them to talk, or maybe play a game, do a jigsaw puzzle. Tomorrow morning Nicole has to see her orthodontist, and Janice has asked me to take them shopping for jeans and shoes; their tiny coastal town has only one small mall. After that, we can get pizza and go to a movie or perhaps bowling, if they're still amused by that at all. Sunday they can sleep late, I'll fix a big dinner and maybe we'll just hang around the house until it's time to go to the airport so I can sneak in some surreptitious adoration of them when they aren't looking.

Finally their flight arrives. They deplane along with a dozen other kids with weekend bags over their shoulders and stereo headphones like big buttons over their ears. They're happy to see me; I'm beaming and I give them bone-crushing hugs. As we walk away from the gate, I've got an arm around each of their shoulders, marveling at how solid and real they are—it has been a month since I've set eyes on them.

"Well," I say, "here's my plan . . ." I run through the schedule and there's what we call "a hue and cry" from them both.

"I've already made plans to spend the night with Aaron tomorrow night, Dad!" complains Keith.

"Jill and I are going skating!" protests Nicole.

"I thought the idea of your coming up here for this weekend was to see me," I say, knowing even as I do that this is not what I really want to say—nobody wants his heart to be so painfully visible on his sleeve. And I know, really, that this was only *my* idea for the weekend.

"Some friends of mine were having a party," says Keith, "and I had to come up here instead of go to it."

My feelings are so hurt I want to say "You should have stayed home then, you little ape!" Luckily, before I can respond in some destructive way, he backs off.

"I mean I didn't mind coming, really, but I want to see my friends here."

"I can understand that."

I *can* understand that—I was twelve once, and I can

remember how, from that point on, the last place in the world I wanted to spend any leisure time was at home and the very last people I wanted to spend it with were my parents, although my teachers would have run a very close second.

But because of our special circumstances, I find it hard to accept. I believe they *need* to spend time with me whether they know it or not and whether they want to or not. It's good for them; it's medicinal or nutritional.

I find it hard to accept because it means that they're growing up, and they need me less now.

They're willing to comply with my plans for the evening, though, and so we go home. Marcia and I put on the spaghetti dinner. I spend the evening following them around like a worshipful younger brother as they watch their TV for a little while then take turns getting on the phone to their friends whom they haven't seen since they moved away. I wedge myself into the interstices of their activity, catch them coming out of the bathroom, pop in just as they're hanging up the phone. Eventually, I sit on one of their beds and jabber away as they unload their backpacks and put their stuff away in their drawers. They seem faintly amused by my persistence. Even though they're twelve, I recite their good-night poem to each of them, just the way I did years ago when they slept in the same room together; they wriggle uncomfortably under this baby stuff ("Aw, Dad!") but seem secretly pleased.

I sleep soundly; it seems I'm smiling blissfully as I sleep, I'm so purged of anxiety: Now, at last, I know they're safe.

The next day we strike out early for the far northern reaches of the city so that Nicole can have her braces adjusted. While Keith and I wait, we pass dog-eared copies of *Sports Illustrated* to one another and make comments about the tropical fish. Just as we're about to relax and settle down to have a conversation about his school, another kid punches three tunes on the orthodontist's jukebox.

We drive to a mall and look for an hour for the right jeans. I'm amenable to this, but it annoys me that they only want a brand that costs almost double what my own cost; if I were a normal parent on a shopping trip, I'd just say "no, they're over my budget," but since I feel more like their grandfather or an uncle who's buying them something for a special occasion I can't show how truly niggardly I feel or how irritated I am that "fashion" has their hooks in them so deeply.

We top off our shopping trip with a stop at Wendy's. By now, Keith is antsy to go to Aaron's, so we drive across town and I drop him off. I give Keith his allowance.

"What are you guys going to do?" I ask. Aaron was the kid with the spiked hair with whom Keith got into trouble in the BB gun incident a while back, and I feel uneasy about the vagueness of these arrangements. I'm thinking, too late of course, that I should have talked to Aaron's mom about this.

"Probably go to the mall or to a movie, dunno for sure, yet."

"Well, I want you to be in by midnight."

"Huh?" He says with a look of disbelief. "Mom lets us stay out until one."

I suspect this isn't true. This is a typical whipsaw deal, whereby they will claim to her that I allow something when I don't in hopes that then *she* will allow it so that they can return to *me* with the information that she will now allow it. Neither of us falls for it. Rather than accuse him of lying, I say, "Well, you're not with your mom now."

"I will be tomorrow!" he says.

"Is that a promise?" I can't resist saying. I am heartsick

that we have both blundered into this fracas; I realize that it is completely irrelevant, anyway—Aaron's mother will decide how late they stay out, and if they're out all night I won't know it unless they get into trouble.

He ignores my insult and starts to get out of the car.

"Wait a minute!"

He gives me a what-now look. I want to grab him and bawl. I want to be his friend. I want to be his daddy.

"I'll come get you about ten tomorrow morning," I tell him.

"Don't come that early, I won't be up yet."

"I'll be here at ten. I'll call before I come so you can *get* up."

As I drive away, I think about how far removed this exchange is from how I dreamed it might be days ago when I was anticipating this visit. I'm in a semipermanent sulk over his having rejected me in favor of Aaron, though I know this is silly.

But I soon forget it; Nicole has brought her skates along, so we drive to a nearby lake that has a jogging track around it and spend a pleasant hour and a half with her skating and me jogging. As we go along, we chat about the ducks, the planes overhead, we talk shamelessly about people who pass us, what they're wearing, what they look like. She's easy to be with today—funny and high-spirited, amenable to suggestion. Having her to myself satisfies my greed for her company, and this time we spend together late in the afternoon restores my equilibrium—things will turn out okay after all. Some day, I think, they'll be grown and will love me and accept me again, they won't be angry any more.

After Marcia and Nicole and I eat at a nearby pizza place, we drive Nicole across town, pick up her friend and drive them to a roller-skating rink in a suburb. I've told her friend's mother that I will pick them up at midnight.

We drive back home and I spend the evening vegetating before the tube. I can't decide if I'm glad or disappointed they're spending the evening with their friends. Maybe both. I'm very tired; I've used two and a half hours of my time today driving through Saturday traffic and my emotional life has been florid, a trip down the Amazon.

At midnight, I get back in my car, drive twelve miles to the skating rink to pick up Nicole and her friend. They're tucked into a cluster of kids hovering about a dark outside corner of the rink; I know enough not to drive right up and honk at them, so I simply park near the front door watching the orange cigarette tips arc in the air as they pitch them away. Seventh grade. Finally, they see me and come get into the car. Nicole wants me to turn on the radio, loud, to a Top 40s station, so I do. She and the friend are clapping and whistling and singing in the back seat, jabbering, slapping each other, laughing—they're like speed freaks, I think, they're so high on being young, on having a good time.

We drop Jennifer off. Nicole climbs into the front seat and, shouting over the radio, tells me about these boys who got into a fight, these girls who poured a Coke down some other girl's neck, how she saw this girl she hadn't seen since fifth grade. At this moment, because she's happy, I consider that maybe I am a good dad, or at least not a bad one. I no longer feel sorry for myself for all the energy I've expended on their behalf during this day.

The next morning, I let her sleep late, but I keep sneaking in to look at her, the way I did when she was only a baby. I start my pot roast cooking, then I call Keith, wake him up, drive to Aaron's house to pick him up. He's groggy and grumpy, but not hostile. When I ask him what they did last night, he says they went to the mall and to a movie.

I don't ask him what time he got home and he doesn't volunteer the information. I'm pleased that he apparently didn't get into any trouble.

By the time we can get dinner on the table, it's after noon; by the time the dishes are cleared away it's time to pack their bags. As I drive them to the airport, I'm feeling very confused. I'm a little relieved that they're going because all my emotional upheaval is exhausting, but I'm also distressed that we didn't do enough together, didn't imprint ourselves upon one another so that we won't forget who we are while we're absent from one another.

I want to make speeches before they go. I want to apologize for all the arguments, want everything to be serene and settled, forgiven, because I have the terrible feeling that I won't see them alive again. This is ridiculous, I tell myself, but there is just enough possibility in it that the thought haunts me and lingers even as I try to shake it off. As we walk up to the gate, I check the monitor for their flight number—392, to Houston—and I try the number out for its possibilities as a newspaper headline or a disaster docudrama title, hoping to get a psychic hint that will settle my mind or give me reason to put them on another flight. "Flight 392 to Houston" sounds, maddeningly, either benign or malign as I turn the phrase over in my head.

They don't want me to make a big fuss when they leave, so I just hug them and say "I love you," and stand waving until they've disappeared down the jetway. Until the plane has landed in Houston fifty minutes later, I'll be tense.

The aftermath leaves me depressed. I expect too much from these visits. It's probably true of my children, too—being depressed, I mean. A friend told me that when his daughter comes to visit him in the summer, "She's always anxious to get here as soon as possible after her school year is out. She'll start calling us long distance and writing us notes several weeks before she comes. She sounds excited about coming, but soon after she arrives a depression sets in."

We engage in too much mythical thinking in our absences from one another. We expect these visits to be more "meaningful," like, say, an episode of *The Waltons* in which a couple of orphans with bruised psyches show up and act pissy for two segments before Grampa gives 'em what-for, Elizabeth charms them, Mary Ellen hugs them, Maw finds them a fine foster home and John Boy says, "And so Huey and Louie discovered on Walton's Mountain what a family truly means." We want to part on Sunday night feeling as if the air has been cleared, that all the good unsaid things were said and that the bad things were wisely left unuttered. We want to have shed tears together in the relief of making up. We need to feel purged.

Most of their visits that spring left me depressed. I would struggle to start anew, over the phone, on Monday, the way you might hope to convince the hostess of Saturday night's party that some insult had been meant to be taken as a joke.

Late that spring, near their thirteenth birthday, disturbing hints seeped into the cracks of my consciousness like a slow water leak: What was that? Somebody found a partly smoked joint on the living room carpet? When? And who? Not mine! they said. The neighborhood kids were a little wild. Then Nicole was said to have drunk a large glass of vodka once when she was alone in the house. Nicole, what's going on? *I just wanted to know what it was like.* Innocent experimentation? Maybe, maybe not. Janice was working long hours and the kids had a lot of time on their hands.

When Janice had to get out of town for a weekend, I

offered to stay in their house to watch over the kids. They lived six hours away from me by car, and the long, solitary drive on Friday gave me ample room to work up a very eager anticipation to see them and to see how they were living. I was worried about them, especially after the recent reports, and it seemed to me that they had grown very incommunicative over the phone.

Their house was, as they had said, on "stilts" and stood in a subdivision about a mile back from the beach; it had a high sundeck overlooking a canal laced with palms, three small bedrooms, with a garage under the house. It had obviously been built to serve as a beach cottage or second home. The location looked to me like every kid's dream— a short walk to the ocean, quiet streets for bike riding.

Keith, I was happy to discover when he came home from school, appeared to be doing well here. His friends had been teaching him to fish and to surf, and he went speeding off to a sandlot baseball game with his glove hooked over the handlebars of his bike. His friends wore rundown sneakers and t-shirts, and when I saw them all with fishing poles over their shoulders the next day they were a living Norman Rockwell picture. He seemed genuinely pleased to see me and to introduce me to his friends. I was proud to be introduced, glad that we could claim kinship before people who mattered to him. At the same time I had the painful perspective of myself as the "absent" dad who shows up once or twice a year to be introduced to people who've been on the scene all along. A visitor, in other words, like a distant relative who's just passing through.

Before Nicole came home, I had time to look around. I found her new ten-speed—this year's Christmas present—in the garage with two flats, the cables and spokes and gears corroded by salt spray and gummed with sand.

Her room was papered with posters and album covers of heavy metal groups on which sets of angry young men clad in black leather and spikes leered and postured. Clothes and papers and used tissues littered the floor; notes from friends were wadded or left lying about where even the most casual eye—and mine was not the most casual—could spot the horrific phrasing of minds just discovering how to relish the vulgar ("So he said give me a blow-job . . ."). Drawings she had done of hollow-eyed, screaming Medusas filled a sketch pad. Tubes and bottles of cosmetics stood on the dresser top, lids lost. I was afraid that if I looked too closely, I'd find vials of illegal pills. Her many Barbies had vanished. *From Barbies to Barbiturates, a Tale of Modern Teendom?*

When she came home, she gave me a perfunctory greeting then disappeared behind her locked door. She played Pink Floyd at top volume ("We don't need no ed-you-kay-shun") and I had to pound on the door and scream to get her attention when I called her to supper.

"Why don't you take better care of your bicycle?" I asked after we had eaten. She just shrugged, went back out into the yard. After a moment the odor of cigarette smoke drifted into the windows.

That night, I took her to a dance program given by some of her classmates, where I met her friends: They all seemed older than her thirteen and wore tight jeans and tight t-shirts, dangling earrings and heavy blue eye shadow—the sort of girls a twenty-one-year-old redneck cruising in his pickup would mistakenly imagine were an easy lay. They all smoked what appeared to be the longest cigarettes they could find, and when I watched them standing around the outside of the auditorium in the pale aura of a streetlamp, their cigarettes were as conspicuous as a baton in a conductor's hand and every bit as busy.

Saturday afternoon, Nicole went out on the sundeck and lay in a bikini on a beach towel. "Would you like to walk down to the beach with me?" I asked. "No," she said, "I just want to get some sun."

She looked very pale; her fair skin has never tanned easily, but in the strong yellow light she looked a cloistered white. Because I thought this might be an opportunity for us to talk, I took her bicycle up onto the sundeck to dismantle it, clean and oil the parts and restore it to use. Sunbathing seemed a blessedly normal activity that reassured me she was still a human child, but when I tried to make conversation, she would only grunt. I had not seen her smile since I had arrived, but I hoped that was due to the discomfort of her braces.

Lying prone, she feigned sleep as I scrubbed rust, salt and sand from gears and cables. I took my time. I remembered how she slept belly down in her playpen, one cheek mashed against the quilt, the other plump and rosy, her cherub's bow-mouth open and little bubbles of drool on her lips, her fat fingers fisted under her chin. And how I could lift her body with my palm across her chest and hold her over my head, and she would giggle and windmill her arms to imitate a bird. Even now she was still well under five feet tall and under one hundred pounds, most of that in leg, but the invisible bell jar she had placed around herself kept me from even trying to hug her. She looked much too young to be smoking, drinking, perhaps experimenting with drugs and running around with girls who had even *heard* the word "blow-job." I knew very little about her daily routine and absolutely nothing about her thoughts and feelings. In only two months she had become an utter stranger to me. The body snatchers had invaded, and my innocent child had been a victim.

The next morning, Sunday, I worked in a stranger's

kitchen preparing a send-off dinner for myself and for them. Janice arrived two hours earlier than expected and I invited her to eat with us. This was the first time in almost three years that we had all sat at a table together. You could hear chewing, forks clinking on plates. Now and then she or I would say something polite, the way you small-talk with a stranger seated beside you on a plane.

Nicole picked at her food then abruptly got up and left the table; only seconds later, Keith asked to be excused, as though the discomfort of the occasion had caused him to recall his formal manners. I had the feeling that they both hated me for the adult's pretense that nothing was different, nothing was wrong. *What right do you have to remind us that you aren't really here?*

I ate far beyond hunger, and when I was finished with my own plate, I ate what was left on theirs.

# NINE

# Medusa Redux

I'm luckier than most divorced men, I thought. Four months after my upsetting visit to their home, they moved back to my city and began the eighth grade.

But soon I learned they were not the same children. They had contracted adolescence. Their clothing smelled of cigarettes; they ran with a pack at shopping malls on Friday nights, where, unbeknownst to their mother and me, their friends smoked dope in dim corners tucked around the loading docks. They attended an inner-city school where an orange van with an ear-shattering stereo system showed up promptly at lunch time to dispense the drug du jour to kids and where small white boys like my son were threatened regularly with an ass-kicking from gangs of low-riders. Half the time Keith was afraid to go to school, but if he learned anything there it was the art of diplomacy: He befriended very large black people.

Nicole's friend "Alicia" lived with her mother except when her mother was on a bender, when she'd go live with her father, a bricklayer, in a trailer park. She was dumb but friendly; rumor had it that she let college boys abuse her sexually. Nicole's friend "Angie" and her friend "Denise" dropped acid, stole credit cards and took off in a "borrowed" car with some eighteen-year-old boys and were caught two states away, for which "Angie" spent a month in juvenile detention. Her friend "Melissa" was always so stoned that friends had to prop her up in class and walk her down the halls, and she eventually spent several weeks in a drug rehabilitation program. They stole from their mothers' purses; they sniffed paint; they watched X-rated movies on cable. They all sneaked out of their houses at night, hitchhiked to wherever it pleased them. They were all a little older than Nicole, and one or two had failed a grade. They all—including my daughter—skipped school with increasing regularity, and one afternoon they wound up at Alicia's mother's apartment and made such a ruckus that a neighbor called the police. Hauled into the principal's office, they laughed it off. They all had parents but very little parenting. They all read *Go Ask Alice* and took it for a model to imitate rather than a warning.

They had no innocence of any kind, but they were all ignorant. They could recite the lyrics to a Van Halen, Scorpions or Motley Crüe album, but they didn't know if El Paso was a city or a state, and the notes they passed among themselves were wholly void of punctuation. Three of her teachers were very concerned about Nicole—she was failing all of her classes. She spent much of one six-week period in at-school detention.

Now she admired criminal behavior. Once, when a driver in front of us made an illegal U-turn, she clapped and said, "All *right*!" She said her friends were "creative" because they were different from the rest of the kids at school. She had become an 85-pound outlaw.

And where was I? Largely in the dark. Seeing her twice

a week or so, I got only hints of the problem through the secretive scrim she had drawn over her life. I saw her alarming report cards; I talked to her teachers, but mostly I was bewildered by her sullenness and her distance.

I was depressed, too. Having them back in town was not turning out as I had hoped. Too many exchanges we had made us seem more estranged rather than closer. After a particularly grueling evening with them, I made notes for a new novel I'd write about a father with kids who do not live with him. It would be framed around a single weekend visitation:

*All-You-Can-Eat Night at Pizza Inn. Or Fat Night— because the buffet attracts white fatties who come to chow down like hogs swathed in polyester stretch pants. He's driven across town during rush hour to bring them here after an argument about where to go which is finally settled by his deciding on a place that his noisiest child, his son, will accept. The place is very hot, with a lot of black dudes wearing plastic bags on their heads, Chicano families with screaming toddlers. One hopelessly incompetent waitress per fifty people. He and his son and daughter are worn out from a long day and are ragged with hunger. His son has his father's metabolism, namely one that makes him short-tempered and irascible when he's hungry, except the son does not believe it when he's been told this.*

*In truth, nobody wants to be here. They don't want to talk to him and he doesn't know what to say to them. It makes him very aware that members of families seldom truly like one another, although they love one another, certainly, and feel obligation and concern for one another's welfare, but they would not pick one another for friends. His kids act as though they're doing him a favor by*

175

*allowing him to drive clear across town to sit in this pizza parlor so they can run off to play video games as soon as their order is in and leave him staring at his place mat; he hasn't bought the right to hear them talk about their lives. The boy and girl have fought in the car on the way here, calling each other "asshole" and "bitch" between the front and back seat while he murmurs, "Don't use words like that."*

*He feels sorry for himself. He's depressed that they cannot have a nice meal with the talk flowing between them easily, with chatter and jokes, like a normal family, which they are no longer. He wants more. Before he picks them up, he yearns to be with them, to protect them, to check on them, to enjoy their company, to be a father and to have them as children, but he isn't with them for five seconds before he's had his feelings hurt, and his disappointment is so keen that he just wants to be away from them again. They disappoint him; he disappoints them.*

*If he were a real father, he would could control their lives even from a distance, force his daughter to stop skipping school and failing her classes, keep his son from having so many "accidents." He feels guilty that he has left their fate to chance and the onerous menace of the ordinary streets. He feels guilty. He's a failure. He would give himself a poor grade for fathering—this is all while staring at the place mat because his kids have deserted him for the Pac Man—yet he takes pride in refusing to give up on the job. He is astonished by the statistics that show how many fathers literally abandon their children. He has always paid his child support and has kept in constant contact with them; he struggles to remain their father even while reality constantly denies that this is true. He would give a year's salary to know for sure that all of his children's agony is not caused by the divorce, that at least some small portion of it is because they are beseiged by, plagued by, adolescence. He's never worried so much about anything as he has about his adolescent daughter in her present condition. What is the cause of unhappiness and rebelliousness in teenage girls? Hormones? The wrong school? The wrong companions? Divorce? Genes? Siblings? A lack of parental attention from either/or father and mother? Movies and records?*

*When their pizza finally comes, he tries to make conversation. "What'd you learn in English today?" His son snorts. "Okay, here it comes," he says. "It's the family talk." Nicole smirks—you want English? "Dad," she asks, "have the words 'fuck' and 'bastard' and 'shit' been around long?" Keith chortles. He could explain the etymologies to her but decides she's only mocking him. "Tell him what happened," his son says, giving the sister a significant look. The daughter shrugs. "This low-rider sent me a note that said 'Lick my dick' so I dumped out a pencil sharpener on his head and so I had to go to Grid." She means detention. "He deserved it," he tells his daughter, suddenly furious with this faceless, nameless low-rider because he exemplifies everything that is wrong with how and where and when his children are, willy-nilly, growing up without his protection.*

*He tells his daughter that he wants her to start going to see a psychologist, and an argument breaks out. The son says this is stupid because counselors are stupid. "You want to know something about her," he says, "just ask me. I know everything there is to know about her." He looks at her. He's got something on her. What is it? He's hostile, belligerent, angry at her and not too pleased to think that her bad behavior is going to earn her some extra attention from his mother and father. "There's nothing wrong with me," says the daughter to the father.*

177

*"This is your idea, and I'll bet you even make Mom pay
for the damn counselor. . . ." Poor "Robert" feels that his
children's adolescence is an ingeniously diabolical punishment for his own sins.*

What a baby! When I wasn't bathing in self-pity, I could
see that we had to get Nicole into counseling. She agreed
to it, partly out of curiosity and partly because she was
worried about herself.

It was called "adolescent reactive adjustment syndrome," which means skipping school, flunking out,
mouthing off, fucking up, taking drugs. Her psychologist,
a pleasant middle-aged woman who seemed intelligent but
who also approached life with a perpetual Happy Face,
gave Nicole a battery of tests about preferences, aptitudes
and attitudes about parents and peers. Part of the testing
involved making up stories to photographs that appeared
to be stills from old movies that had been reshot using a
gauze over the lens to make them fuzzy and fantasylike:

1. *A man is looking out of the frame while a woman clutches
at his bicep.* The story behind this picture, according to
Nicole, is that the man is leaving the woman, his wife, for
another woman. The other woman may be involved with
the mob and needs to be rescued, but the man cannot tell
his wife that. He leaves anyway. Years later he comes back
to apologize, but the wife has remarried. There is a child,
who is now traveling around playing with a rock band (he
doesn't know anything about that—he listens to jazz). He
gets so discouraged that he goes off and buys a winery,
becomes an alcoholic and dies when his car runs into a
parked car.

I didn't need a degree to understand the basic thrust of
this, how she seemed to make excuses for me (the other
woman needs to be rescued) and needed to acknowledge

her mother's suffering yet still not blame me for it (the man can't tell his wife that he "has" to go). And my punishment by this angry little goddess—I reform too late to restore my family, my child is alienated from me, I deteriorate and die. What tormented me about her interpretation was how it showed she still loved me and was groping to justify my actions, yet she was furious under it all.

2. *A girl is in a tree looking down onto a sidewalk where another girl is running by.* "Only the girl in the tree is real," says Nicole. The girl below is only an image the girl in the tree has of herself. She's wondering what she will be like in the future. The girl below is running toward the future, but she's also "running away from something and she doesn't know what it is, something is chasing her."

3. *A girl is bending backward and looking over her shoulder while a man smoking a pipe is leaning over a sofa toward her.* This is taking place "either in the morning or late at night because they look tired. The man is saying something or he is replying to something the girl has said. It's her father, and they are having an argument. But the father then goes away in order to avoid an argument. . . . It only goes to show that you can't get anywhere with someone who thinks older means wiser."

After several weeks, the counselor concluded that Nicole was suffering from low self-esteem and advised us to accentuate the positive. But whenever we gave Nicole a compliment she would sneer and, world-weary, would say, "You're just saying that because she told you to say it to make me feel good."

What none of us knew was that Nicole was stoned all the time. Apparently upon arriving at school each day, she'd load up in the restroom with whatever drugs were available—speed, grass, Valium—then go blotto through her classes. She even attended her therapy sessions half under the influence of a chemical moon. Drugs didn't make her noticeably high or low; rather, they made her walk about like something waterlogged and bobbing barely above the surface of reality; she was "distant" and "moody," precisely how textbooks describe adolescents.

Several times she sneaked out at night to join her friends. Grounded, she would closet herself in her room amid the tornadic blasts of the stereo and do version after version of that black-and-white Medusa face I had first seen her draw when she was living in the house near the beach. The figure had wild, electrified hair, a square jaw, large hollow eyes without pupils and a howling mouth; it was half Fury, half vampiress.

In April Nicole took a horse tranquilizer (PCP) with the street name "angel dust." It scrambled her brains. She began hearing voices that told her to hurt herself; she believed they were real. They belonged to characters to whom she gave fablelike names such as "Bendikak." They looked like trolls when they popped into the frame of her vision. Some told her to do "good things" and some "bad things."

Her counselor advised hospitalization. While we looked for the right place, she was "sentenced" to stay at my house, out of reach of her friends so my wife and I could keep close watch over her. She was furious and deadly silent. She kept drawing that face and broke off only to construct an odd tableau. Acting obsessed, she found an old Frisbee in the alley, washed it and turned it rim up; she cut out a page from a magazine depicting a winter woods scene and attached it along one side of the Frisbee's rim like a backdrop; she glued silver glitter to the floor of the disk. I asked what it was. "Snow," she grunted. She next fashioned a small skirted figure out of tin foil, a girl whose arms were spread in a cruciform position, and mounted it on the glitter-covered "stage." Then she dug a clear plastic glass out of the trash and glued it in place mouth-down over the figure. She scissored an arm about the size of her little finger out of white paper and glued the shoulder joint to the top of the glass so that the arm waved slightly with air currents. It was as if the girl inside the glass had an extra, detached limb that had managed to penetrate to the outside of this otherwise unyielding surface.

It was an eerie little sculpture. It would easily have illustrated an edition of Sylvia Plath's *The Bell Jar*.

Going into the hospital was scary for her. A part of her welcomed it because she needed help and knew it would be an interesting experience, but, even though she had toured the ward before being admitted officially, the moment she realized that she would be kept behind locked doors, she balked: She couldn't eat or drink what she wanted to! And why were they taking away all her belongings? This was insane—she couldn't smoke unless she earned the right and then only with permission and in specified areas!

They took away cosmetics vials made from glass or hard plastic so that they couldn't be broken and their sharp edges used to cut herself or their contents ingested; They informed her that she would not be allowed phone calls or visits from her friends; that she would have almost no time to herself. She would attend school on the ward but the rest of her time would be devoted to activities planned for her by other people who, to her mind, seemed to relish making lists of absurd rules, such as not allowing her to take an aspirin on her own.

It wasn't a hospital—it was a jail!

That night I slept soundly for the first time in two months. It was not only relief that she was safe—the worry, anxiety and lost sleep had equalized my guilt for having been responsible for her condition, and hospitalizing her gave me a sense of accomplishment. I had earned the right to sleep.

Her mother, her teachers, her brother and her case workers and I saw her constantly. We had to learn to deal with the personality that had been buried under that avalanche of chemicals. She was being treated for depression by nonchemical therapies. It was the opinion of the staff that she had been suffering from depression and had been treating her own condition with street drugs. She had been numb for so long that when her feelings were allowed to flow, the wildly oscillating nature of emotional upheaval alarmed her. She deeply resented our "help." She broke into tears over little things. We had stormy, screaming arguments over her smoking, over what was right behavior for someone her age, over rules and expectations, over having visits from her friends. Scuttlebutt had it that one planned to bring her a bit of acid on the sly or was going to mail it to her dissolved on stationery.

After ten days or so, she made plans for a weekend out of the hospital. That precipitated a typical argument during my visit on Thursday night. Prior to my arriving, I knew that she had recently earned the privilege of accepting a specified number of phone calls. I guessed that she had been using them to make plans for her weekend. I was expecting to have to fight with her about these. Later, I gave the following report to the doctor:

> When I got here, Nicole was glum and looked depressed. She denied it, said she was tired and had a headache. We chatted about her day, she volunteering short phrases in a listless and irritated way. She then asked if she would be allowed to see her friends if she went home for the weekend. I said I didn't know yet, but that if she were,

*it would be under conditions that she would have to agree to. "Like adult supervision?" she asked with a sneer. I said yes. She said that she wanted to go to a party at her boyfriend's house on Saturday night that her friends were going to throw for her, and I told her it was out of the question. This caused an argument about whether or not she could be trusted. She launched into a tirade, the gist of which seemed to be this: Nobody knows her mind except her, not me, not her mother, not the doctors or any of the staff. Only she can solve her own problems. She doesn't really have any problems; the problems are ours in dealing with her—she's only here because she made a mistake in mixing drugs—a pharmaceutical error, as it were. She can take some drugs every now and then if she damn well pleases! She doesn't need drugs. We should be able to trust her to not take drugs. She can work her own way out of her problems by sitting down and thinking about them. She should be allowed the freedom to see her friends because she can learn to control herself and make her own choices only if she is allowed to make those choices; yes, she might choose to do things that are harmful to her, but it's her life!*

With each visit, there were new, recent renderings of the Medusa taped to her wall.

But as the weeks went by, she grew more sunny, witty even; she had a kooky sense of humor that endeared her to the staff. She made close friends with other girls who had similar problems. Some days she was more like the person I had known, and had all but forgotten, before she had moved away to the coast. She grew hospital wise and expressed a desire to someday be a psychologist. "I acted out in group today," she said, "I didn't handle things well."

In the parents' group, I discovered the obvious truth

that those who have your problems can make you feel better. We were a motley crew who had nothing in common but our troubled children. It was a writer's paradise. There was an aging biker with tattoos who wore jeans and a Harley-Davidson t-shirt; he had had drug problems and had given over the care of his six-year-old son to his mother, a sweet-tempered, elephantine nurse who couldn't handle the boy's "wildness." The child had been kicked out of a dozen day-care centers and the first grade. The father attended our sessions with his mother, held his tongue for two weeks then one day he slumped forward and moaned, "I've been such a lousy father!"

Samantha's mother and stepmother came in tandem and sat side by side. The mother was a tall, friendly, raw-boned country gal in a brunette Farrah Fawcett winged harido ten years out of style. She spoke in a voice disturbingly reminiscent of Gomer Pyle's. The stepmother sported the same winged brunette hairdo and had similar though more refined facial features and a quiet, genteel voice, all of which gave me the impression that the father/husband whom we never set eyes on had been working on a rough draft when he married the mother and had taken the second wife as a more polished version.

Connie's father wore plaid vested suits and had the bland, rabbit-pink face of a PTL Club preacher, an impression he only reinforced when he claimed to have turned his daughter's problems over to God. His wife wore silk blouses and tailored slacks and might have been a beauty queen at Baylor in the early Fifties. I thought they felt they really shouldn't be there, and I detested them for that. They had two other daughters they had not had a moment's trouble with, but Connie had come from school with the word "drugs" carved into her forearm with a knife and they had discovered a marijuana cigarette in her purse.

None of their friends had had these problems with *their* children. They had no idea where Connie was learning to say such things as "Piss off!" They had done everything right. "She's got everything a kid could want," the father said. "We have good values." They were clearly concerned that Connie would be associating with problem children here at the hospital, and they were also very worried about what their friends would think should they learn that Connie was here, although what the mother actually said was, "We haven't told any of our friends that Connie's here so she won't have to feel embarrassed when she comes home."

I snorted. I relished their discomfort. I hated them for being so innocent; I hated them because they represented what I yearned to be: a guiltless parent. I acted up; I told them that obviously something had gone wrong some-where—I took a perverse pleasure in reminding them that the world they had constructed so carefully out of conventional "decency" was obviously too narrow to contain and control real life. They could not pinpoint a cause to blame, although from session to session they would try out a new theme, a kind of "cause of the week." One week it was school (Connie attended public school in a middle-class suburb but would not be sent back), once it was television, once it was moral corruption in society—during our sessions, John Belushi died and the De Lorean case was in the papers. For two sessions it was her friends, and for part of one session it was, for God's sake, rock and roll and punk fashion.

They were concerned, they were bewildered, they were angry, they were tormented by their own weather-vane churning from cause to cause to set their minds at rest. They wanted to know that she could get "well," but so long as they didn't know what made her "bad," they could have no confidence in the treatment. They believed in

185

progress, in perfectibility, in medical science, and they worried that they coudn't reap the rewards of progress if they didn't "qualify" by having a case that could be clearly understood: Connie's disease, so to speak, might be too rare for a cure to be known.

I should have been sympathetic, but it was hard. They couldn't locate a cause for Connie's trouble. I knew exactly what had caused Nicole's.

Yet, as it turned out, my presuming complete responsibility for Nicole's condition was an arrogance in itself. Looking about, I saw a teacher, a biker, a nurse, a secretary, an insurance salesman, a housewife, a lawyer; I saw that we were raising our children as unmarried singles, as never-divorced couples, as divorcees, as single fathers, as grandmothers. Our group was a veritable smorgasbord of variations on the human family. But, most importantly, I realized that difficulties such as Nicole's happened to "nice" folks such as Connie's parents.

*So maybe I was not altogether to blame!*

Since Connie's parents had unwittingly provided this revelation, I felt more kindly toward them, like a veteran of wars I knew they would never have to fight. We who have abandoned, deserted, divorced or otherwise left our children, or only moved out of their homes, live with the burden of guilt that makes judgment difficult. When something goes wrong, we immeditely go for our own jugular. But nobody knows for certain why kids go haywire: The causes could be emotional, spiritual, psychological, genetic, social or chemical. In Nicole's case, her problems were diagnosed as stemming from a cyclical depression that was partly physiological and partly environmental; it was a combination of a genetic disposition to depression coupled with adolescence and the pervasive sadness over the breaking up of her family. My leaving was not a necessary or even sufficient cause for Nicole's problem, though it was certainly a contributory one. My job now was to minimize the damage. Whether I was in their home or not, I had better pay as close attention as I possibly could to how they were doing.

The night before Nicole left the hospital, the staff and patients held a talent show on the ward for the parents. An eight-year-old girl with spectacles so thick they made her eyes look like those of a species of bottom-dwelling fish played "Memories" on the piano one note at a time; Shelley, Nicole's sixteen-year-old roommate and friend, sang "Run for the Roses" because Dan Fogelberg was her favorite composer and horses her favorite animal (the wall over her bed was papered with her drawings of horses and unicorns). A squat twelve-year-old with a perpetual scowl announced she was going to do an aerobics routine to music, then after several false starts, she finally did jumping jacks through the entire length of Michael Jackson's "Beat It." She got hysterical and exhausted about halfway through; her face turned purple, her jaw clenched, her features were contorted as if an invisible wrestler had a claw-hold on her face, and we all feared she would drop dead before the song ended. Using the same Michael Jackson tape, Samantha and Norma, twelve and thirteen respectively, came out clad in little white short-shorts, high heels, tight t-shirts and too much makeup and did a Solid Gold-style dance number that made Connie's Baptist father blush. A girl with long blonde hair played a flute solo, and Nicole and a teenage boy did an old pantomime shtick about a wad of bubble gum that gets passed from place to place.

Since Nicole was leaving the next day, this was like a graduation ceremony to me. We were all poised on the edge of an unknown future, and it made me nervous— would this have had any lasting beneficial effect? Nicole had developed a camaraderie with many fellow patients, that special bond shared by those who have endured extraordinary circumstances together, and she was close to many of the staff. During the evening, I saw her hug at least a dozen people, incluing me; when she was not performing, she sat with me in the audience and discussed the other performers' problems with a kind of earnest, religious hush, as if she were engaged with the doctors in helping that person get well.

Nicole got out of stir with walking papers that pronounced her sound again, for which I am immensely grateful to the staff. For a while she kept drawing renditions of that Medusa, though each successive version seemed to represent something like stages of evolution out of the slime.

One of the last she colored with pastel pencils; the woman has blonde hair and high cheekbones with a slight peach flush. Her mouth is closed, and she has feminine lips. She isn't smiling, but the curve of the lips suggests repose; her jaw has softened, and she has large, pale blue eyes with curving lashes. One brow goes up, the other down in some faint intimation of melancholy. The old gal seems human now.

# TEN

# Now and Then

"What were her friends wearing?"

"Tight Jordache jeans, tight sweaters," she says, then grins. "Typical slut-type stuff."

"How about Denise?"

She squints, cocks her head, thinking. "Some kind of jumpsuit. It just made her look more pregnant." Critically she dissects a stuffed noodle from her wonton soup with the edge of a spoon then says, "What was really weird was that Angie and I and Alicia were all wearing dresses like a bunch of grown-up ladies."

We're sitting in a Chinese restaurant on a Monday night. Monday's been our "night for sure" lately. I picked her up from school, took her to her therapist's, and later I'll help her with a government assignment at the library. We talk about everything, about nothing, though sometimes she won't talk at all. She always stays mum about her sessions with her therapist. Although I'm aware that she sometimes talks about the divorce, more often she uses her time to discuss school, her future, her boyfriend.

It's hard to wedge myself into her schedule even though she's only minutes away; she works Sundays as a restaurant hostess and likes to keep her nights free for her homework and her boyfriend. These Monday nights, though, I feel a little as if we're dating. I flirt; I make jokes; or, unfortunately, I wind up giving lectures I've stored up over the week: "I wish you would stop smoking, especially Marlboros." I nag too much about homework. She makes decent grades and she recently got an invitation to join the National Arts Honors Society, but I always imagine that my nagging could motivate her to do better. I forget that sometimes it's best for an absent father to drop the pose of authoritarian patriarch in favor of being a brotherly confidant.

Tonight we're talking about her old pals whom she recently saw at a baby shower for the first time in a year. When Nicole first got out of the hospital, we kept her away from her Gang of Four in her old neighborhood, partly by forbidding her from seeing them and partly by logistics: Janice sold her old house and bought another in a neighborhood across town. After Nicole got out of the hospital, Janice rented a van and had taken her and Keith and a friend on a trip to the Grand Canyon, Yosemite Park and San Francisco, and I had flown to Los Angeles to drive the homebound leg, with stops at Disneyland, Juarez and Carlsbad Caverns. She had started ninth grade immediately thereafter at a high school for the performing arts. Over the course of that year she received a lot of attention and kept herself straight, developed her talents as an artist and fell in love with her school.

During that time she kept asking, "Can I see my friends?" We kept putting her off. She was straightforward and candid. "I know we did a lot of bad things, Dad," she said. "And I know that being with them wasn't good for me in a lot of ways. But I've never felt so close to a group since then, and I really miss them." She understood that it was unlikely that they would ever all be friends again; they didn't live in her neighborhood any more and didn't attend her school. Eventually, the idea of her attending a reunion really didn't alarm me because I had come to trust her strength.

Since Nicole had last seen her, Denise had turned sixteen, had dropped out of school, had gotten pregnant and was living with her boyfriend. Angie, who had dropped acid with Denise and had taken the joy ride on stolen credit cards, had moved out of her mother's house, too. She now lived with her boyfriend, a construction laborer, worked at a Fotomat kiosk and was attending night school. Alicia had been living with relatives in a small town not too far away, where she had been attending high school like a normal person and she had astonished everyone by declaring that she planned to become a dentist. Also present were a new friend of Denise's, a seventeen-year-old girl who had a three-month-old infant she brought along to the shower, and two other friends whom Nicole didn't know—they were the ones wearing "slut-type stuff."

"So what did you ladies do in your dresses, just sit around talking about babies?" I joked. In my own manipulative, parental way, I was trying to pry enough information to assess what conclusion she had come to from seeing Denise as a pregnant drop-out. Maybe I wanted to reassure myself that the lesson was obvious to Nicole.

"It was weird," she said. She laughed. "It wasn't exactly like a shower. For one thing, we couldn't get Angie's boyfriend to leave—he didn't seem to understand what this was."

"So what did you do?"

"We opened presents and went walking down to the park, and then we came back and all fixed dinner while

Denise and her friend talked about babies. Some other people came over that I didn't know, and Angie and I and Alicia went off in another room and looked at some old pictures and talked."

"What about?"

"About Denise some. You know, she used to dance and laugh a lot, and now she just was sitting back on the sofa and kind of smiling every now and then. She seemed unhappy being pregnant. It seemed like she and her friend with the baby were pretending or acting like half their life was over and that they'd already experienced everything that anybody could possibly experience. They kept talking about hard times and how hard their lives were. And then when the party was about over, Denise's boyfriend came to get her and they got into a fight. Angie said they fight all the time."

"How do you feel about all that?"

She knew what I wanted to hear, but she was not going to be my dupe. "Well, I was glad to see my friends and be with them. I could tell that being apart had made us become more our own selves. I remember how I always thought Alicia was just goofy and then she said she wanted to be a dentist. Angie seems very smart to me now—she's not doing any drugs, and she says she's much happier not living at home. She's going to finish school even if she has to work days and go nights."

Okay, I thought, I'm going to have to beg. "I mean what did you feel about seeing Denise pregnant?"

She gave me a cocky grin. "Well, of *course* I wouldn't want to be a pregnant drop-out, Dad!"

Now that she's through with her soup, she gives me a grin. "Got a quarter, Pop?"

This is not a non sequitur. She wants to check in with Zack, her boyfriend. I know she's got change in her purse for a phone call, but she's grinning so winningly I can't refuse her. She's being charming, alluding to how Keith used to squeeze quarters out of me when we went out to eat in the old days. It makes me feel good to cough it up; playing my part in the ritual, knowing the inside joke, makes me feel closer to her. I do feel a twinge of jealousy, though, to think that she can't be with me for a couple of hours wihout thinking of Zack. At fifteen, she's turned out to be very pretty and dresses herself with flair in the bag-lady style students at her school have adopted. Over a pink blouse gathered at her neck by an antique brooch she wears an old burgundy cardigan that belonged to my father. I envy Zack her undivided attention.

Zack is twenty-one. You ask me should I or her mother allow this and I would say no, we shouldn't, but we do. For one thing, we like her boyfriend—he's short, red-haired, freckled and looks much younger than his years, and when they're standing side by side decked out in their thrift-shop-chic, they look like elves who are down at the heels. They're cute together. He speaks English, loves music, is a drummer but works as a professional photographer. He still lives at home; he could stand a lot more formal education, but he's sensitive, fairly articulate and is always willing to talk; he's friendly, presentable, sociable; he doesn't appear to drink or take drugs, and he's nuts about Nicole. Now that I'm used to the idea, his being twenty-one bothers me less, and I can easily imagine a worse situation, from my point of view, such as her dating a sixteen-year-old jerk who drinks and likes to show off his driving skills.

Zack is not an accident. He came into her life precisely as Keith was moving in with me, so Zack is partly her father, partly her brother, partly her boyfriend. It worries me that her choice of Zack is so obviously an expression of her continuing need for me and Keith. Though she and her brother quarreled frequently, Nicole admitted that Keith's moving to my house hurt her: "When you left you broke up the family, Dad," she said, "but there was still the three of us. But when Keith went to live with you, it only left me and Mom—so the original family's now cut in half, and that's all I've got left."

I insist that she hasn't really "lost" us at all. At the time we made this rearrangement, she seemed nonchalant about it. But how many times does it have to happen before I realize that this child demonstrates her fear, anxiety and pain by acting nonchalant? We invited her to discuss it with her counselor, whom she has been seeing off and on as an out-patient at the hospital over the last two years.

Still, even now she will not admit to being angry about this, because that's admitting to having been made vulnerable by having cared. And when her seasonal cycles of depression roll around and set in like bouts of the flu, she stews on this and on everything that is, or has been, happening. An overcast moves across the sky of her normally sunny moods, and it will hang there for weeks. These cycles are like slow tides, predictable (October and April) and connected in some enigmatic way both to chemical seepage deep in her conduitry and to events above the decks, as it were.

Last fall, at the onset of one of these cycles, she spent two weeks with us while Janice was out of town. When she comes under the moon of this affliction, her behavior changes—she gets passive, moody, balky and surly—and I'm always perplexed as to how to deal with her: I never know whether her behavior requires correction or medical attention. I play the angry parent part of the time and punish her for being "childish," then that seems terribly stupid and it seems she's acting badly because she's depressed, not because she's bad.

During that stay, she was sullen and uncommunicative.

I believed she was angry with Marcia for having stolen me away from her mother, angry with me for having left her mother and her, angry with me for having taken Keith away from her, angry with Keith for having betrayed her and her mother by coming to live with us, and angry at her mother for making this upheaval necessary. She came silently to meals, sat with her eyes on her plate and asked to be excused as soon as she had finished. She didn't volunteer anything about her feelings or her life or even her day's activities, and she made no effort to integrate herself into our lives. She wouldn't watch television, play games or even converse with us; she didn't offer to help around the house, and, more significantly, she would steadfastly refuse to ask any of us for anything directly.

The only real contact I had with her over this two-week period had to do with our conflicts over rules about the household and her curfew. We asked her to be tidy, but she refused on the grounds that she wasn't like us—to her, following our rules about picking up after yourself was not a matter of courtesy; as the *artiste* she reserved the right to be sloppy and "creative," and we had no right to impose our values on hers. Or she would just "forget" to do as we asked, which made it clear that what we asked was not important enough to remember. When she asked me to iron a blouse for her one busy morning before school, I did it but also told her she needed to organize herself better, that I didn't mind ironing the night before but I didn't want to suddenly face an unscheduled ten-minute chore in the morning. She half-heartedly agreed to comply, but the next morning she said, "I guess you wouldn't want to iron a skirt for me, would you?" and I said no. I could tell she was angry—she adopted that cool and passive air of aloof superiority that told me she thought my "program" for organization, as she once called it, was a far inferior plan for life than going with the flow, that she was very proud of being a spontaneous person.

She couldn't allow herself to be under any obligation to us. She was failing algebra but when I suggested to her that Marcia would be willing to tutor her, she said, "Sure, that would be okay, if she really wants to do it. Does she really *want* to do it?" Nicole was willing to be tutored by Marcia if Marcia would ask, so that Marcia's tutoring would be something that Nicole could "give" Marcia. Marcia would then owe her, in other words, for having been allowed to tutor her. "She's willing to help you," I repeated. "But you'll have to ask." She never did.

One Saturday, she asked me, "You wouldn't want to take me to work at two would you?"

"If you ask me, I'll do it," I said.

"Jesus! What's the big deal?"

"If you want me to give you a ride to work then I have a right to have you acknowledge that I'm doing this for you."

"That's the way *you* think! But I'm not like you, and you might as well quit trying to change me!"

We argued; she claimed that she asked that way so people could easily refuse the requests if they didn't want to do them. But I said the real reason she wouldn't ask directly was that she wouldn't have to acknowledge that someone had done something for her. She wouldn't be obliged to reciprocate or even to say thank you. If we volunteered to help her, then she didn't owe us anything—we helped her only to please ourselves, and by allowing herself to be the object of our attention, she had performed an act of charity.

I held my tongue and didn't say this—that she wanted to think she was totally independent because dependency

196

is especially galling if it is upon people at whom one is angry.

I also didn't air my deepest grievance against her—that in the six years since I had moved out of her house, she had never called just to find out how I was feeling or what I was doing, and that the calls she initiated were always requests for services, usually couched in the circumlocutory language we were arguing about.

In the heat of any argument, she was likely to say, "You don't know anything about me or about my life!" My essential ignorance is a fact, but it's not a fault—I can't know anything about someone who never volunteers any information and who turns aside any questions.

When she's depressed, she demonstrates all the classic passive-aggressive earmarks of the grudge-holding personality: She borrows things then loses them, she fails to keep appointments, she constantly "forgets" whatever you ask her to remember. She expects you to read her mind and then blames you for not knowing what she wants or feels or thinks. She's hypersensitive and will turn a small, seemingly harmless comment over in her mind for days before ever mentioning in even an off-handed way how it struck her. When she's depressed, everything about her says, "I have something against you but I'm not about to tell you what it is because I want to hold on to it."

But then this cloud lifts and another personality emerges. We have pretty good times, she and I, just talking, and then our conflicts seem like normal ones between fathers and teenage daughters and I can take them in stride. When I'm only a "parent" with "teenagers," I don't feel as alone. Thinking of myself as a "normal" parent allows me latitude to remove the ill consequences of my acts, of believing that the time since the divorce has healed some wounds.

*197*

It seems presumptuous to feel that what I did when she was nine years old has determined every minute motion of her mind since then. She even gets annoyed sometimes when I analyze something she has done by alluding to the divorce; it's as if she thinks it's arrogant of me to think that what's happening to her now must always be attached to something I did in the past.

But then sometimes she penetrates right to the heart of this, quite innocently and not from an intent to hurt me. We were talking one day about her future, about whether she should become an artist or a psychologist, and I said, "Well, there's your love life to consider, too."

"Oh, I think I'll just live with somebody," she said. "I don't think I'll get married."

"Why not?"

"Because then I might have kids and just get divorced."

I worry about her future because the marriage she was born to serves as a bad example. I worry because her unresolved anger will likely hinder her happiness. Naturally I'd like to be forgiven, but I'm mostly concerned that carrying these grievances about will damage her life; I know she can never be truly happy until she forgives me and quits being angry.

Our waiter brings the orders before she comes back, but just as I've lifted the metal covers off the pepper steak and cashew chicken to serve them, she slides into the booth.

"Sorry I took so long," she says.

For a while we chat at random while we eat. She asks about my upcoming trip to France and says, "Be sure to bring me back something."

I say, "How about a barbeque apron? Or a t-shirt that says 'My Daddy Went to France and I Only Got This Lousy T-Shirt'?"

"I was thinking maybe a waterbed."

Then we're quiet. I watch her pick the cashews and the chicken chunks out of her food and push the crunchies to the side. She has a teenager's palate, which means that she will eat some "grown-up" foods and will experiment here and there, but invariably every meal will contain a small demonstration of juvenilia: With her cashew chicken, she's drinking Sprite.

Because I have been working on the part of this book dealing with our life in the Midwest, where she started school, I ask her what she remembers about this period.

"I remember it seemed like a good time because there weren't any problems," she says.

"Problems?" I wonder, as always, if she means the divorce.

"Yeah, like grown-up problems. Decisions. I think I liked it because I got to get out into the world, go to school. I was real insecure, though, come to think of it. I used to cheat at coloring!" She laughs.

"How can you cheat at coloring?"

"It was in kindergarten. The teacher would give us paper and crayons and tell us to draw or color something, and I would always get up from my seat after a while to go ask her something but really I wanted to check to see what colors everybody else was using. And I remember the time you and Mom were going to make me and Keith start riding the school bus to school, and so we went out to wait for it, but when it came I was so scared that after Keith got on it, I ran back to the house and hid in the back of the car so you guys would have to take me to school. And one time I ran away from home with just my socks on. And then I remember how you used to get mad at me and Keith because after we played in the basement we wouldn't turn the light off down there when we came up. You thought it was because we didn't want to mind you, but it was really because we were scared to be down there in the dark."

"I thought you said you liked this place."

"Oh, well, yeah, the good stuff. I had this secret tree in the backyard that was just my place and nobody else's. I could climb up in it and look at the bugs crawling around on the limbs and the leaves and find cocoons and stuff. I could take your binoculars up there and watch the big kids across the street playing in their fort. I could just sit up there and think, pretend I was Alice in Wonderland—that was my favorite story in those days."

Laughing, she remembers how when she and her brother were playing outside in the yard, right in the middle of a game he would stop for a few seconds to pee behind the bushes. "And I remember watching *Space 1999* on our old TV that only got two channels, one with only the sound and the other with only the picture, and then we got a new one and watched *Donnie and Marie*. You used to make me so mad—you used to tease me about liking the little fat one. Jimmy? And we had our first real record player, our first record. It was 'Midnight's All Right,' and we danced to it in our room. And once Uncle Michael came to stay for a while. He taught me how to do collages."

"Yes, for a month."

"And I remember the winter it snowed so much."

I do, too. I make a mental note to write about it. Then, only moments later it seems, while I'm still eating, she asks, in a whine, "May I be excused?"

This is a euphemistic expression. She means, "Will you give me permission to let me be rude to you so that I can go out to the car and smoke a cigarette?" I've told her she can smoke in front of me though not in my house, but she knows that I hate to see her smoking and that I'll nag her, so she prefers to avoid the hassle. I don't know which I prefer—that she "hide" it from me or do it in front of me. I've never been one of those extraordinary, understanding parents who reserves judgment simply so a child will feel at ease about revealing whatever mischief he or she's been up to. Janice is; she believes in "Keeping the lines of communication open" so that Nicole can come talk to her without fear of immediate condemnation or punishment. I admit that Janice's method is superior.

I could say, "No, you may not leave the table yet because the adults aren't finished." I resent that it means more to her to get nicotine into her bloodstream than to spend time with me. I believe that it's still important for her to see me frequently even though she imagines she's outgrown a need for a daddy, but who wants to be kept company by a captive companion?

"Beg," I say. "On your knees."

"Please."

"Admit that you're a thrall of the American tobacco companies."

"I admit it."

"Admit you're a slave, a junkie, that whenever they feel like it they can get—what is it—a dollar-thirty now? from you, just like the Mafia or something."

"Okay, okay, okay!" she grins sheepishly.

She takes my keys and leaves. She's left a lot of good crunchy vegetables in the cashew chicken. In her absence, I polish off that dish and go back to work on my pepper steak. I get a cheap high out of all the MSG and continue meditating on our sujet du jour; recollections of good and bad times past.

It's odd that Nicole recalls that period in the Midwest with fondness because I hated the place. Number One on my own Best Memories chart predates that period, and since Nicole's not present to hear it, I replay it for my own enjoyment.

It's the Time I Showed Them the Ocean. We went to the beach at Corpus Christi, on Padre Island National Seashore, to be exact. It's the one vacation we all took together that wasn't spent driving to our parents' homes and dividing up for obligatory visits.

It happened the summer Janice and the kids, who were then five, moved down from Missouri to finish the last quarter of my year-long fellowship at Paisano.

Hey! I said one night to Janice. Our children have never seen the ocean! Let's go to the beach!

So we packed up the VW van with enormous enthusiasm. I cut a child-sized board from plywood to lay across the two front seats for one kid to sleep on at night; then we fixed a platform in the rear for the rest of us. Loaded up the old red metal cooler—which I guess was not old then; it was bought expressly for this trip—took a first-aid kit that included Adolph's Meat Tenderizer as a balm for jellyfish stings, inner tubes, sunblock, a big orange five-gallon water jug, a borrowed Coleman cookstove and lantern, odds and ends, and lit out for Corpus, six hours away. Now that I think of it, the tarp was new, too, and I went out and cut some long thin saplings and stripped their bark to use them for shelter poles.

I was itchy to get back to the sea. I was born in Corpus and had lived near the coast until I was about four. Our family photo album has a section devoted to Corpus, and many snapshots show me playing on the beach. So on the drive down, I anticipated seeing it again myself and introducing my children to it, taking a weird kind of double pride and pleasure in this, once as a guide who had known it first, twice as a father giving it to his children.

We arrived mid-afternoon at Padre after stopping on the outskirts of Corpus for food and ice. Next maybe we found a good spot for camping in a bay of sand among the dunes that opened out onto the beach. The kids instantly ran down to the water while I erected our shelter using the big orange tarp and the skinned saplings. Maybe it was that way, anyway. Maybe that happened next. It could have been that I kept them from going to the water until some adult could accompany them—there were safety lectures to give on undertow and these poisonous jellyfish. I do know that at some point I kept them from going down by themselves, maybe at this point maybe later. Maybe I ripped off my shoes on stopping the van and we all ran down to the surf and cooled our feet in it and dug our toes in the sand. No matter when we went we always returned to camp with sticky black patches on our soles from the tar balls coughed up by offshore wells, patches only alcohol would dissolve and clean.

My trouble is that I can't string the memories together in their proper chronology because one memory doesn't seem to lead to the next the way events in a story or in life do. Each memory is separate from every other as to its time or position in the chronology over those three—or was it four?—days; they are only images, pictures with the ocean as a backdrop, like still photographs that move but not *toward* something else, like those humorous lapel buttons that have a different message when you shift your eyes slightly when looking at them.

The images cluster, drawn to centers. There's sunlight, for instance, very warm but diffused by the moisture in the air—there's a white haze around the sun—so it feels as though the heat radiates from all about us. I felt it in the top of their blonde heads when I put my palm there. "Go get your hats." If I take off my sunglasses, the light is blinding. I remember lying down on the beach in a shallow trench they dug for me and their trying to cover me up with wet sand while I hollered supposedly in horror of being forced into suspended animation in a cool damp place. I remember Nicole had on a red bathing suit and Keith was wearing brown shorts; they were both already tanned from days on the creek at the ranch, so they had sunscreen only on their ears and noses. They put a straw hat over my face; in the hollow it formed I could smell grass and sweat, and the sun made the air there hot, but it was quiet and still. When I opened my eyes under the hat everything was light gold. Keith and Nicole made cackling mad-scientist noises while tossing the cool sand onto my body. I was afraid they'd get too tired to finish the job. Later I washed off in the surf and lay on a towel on my stomach, feeling the yellow hot light drying the water and salt and sand on my skin so that when I moved, the skin on my back pinched and creaked. Another picture I have is from a standing position, looking down at their heads as they walk in the inch-deep surf and seeing their faces reflected in the shimmering glassy water, then the sun sharply glinting off the water and blinding me.

At first they were shy of the water. They went running along the beach, which was covered by a shifting sheet of foam-edged surf, and their feet went *split split split,* while mine went *splat.* They sat with their legs spread and let the surf come rushing up the sand to swirl around their hips and make them shriek; then they ran into ankle-high water and kicked at it to make big splashes. Then I thought they were ready. I took each in hand and we waded into the surf. I kept my eye out for the jellyfish that would loom suddenly riding the crest of a wave about to roll over us, especially the dangerous and eye-catching Portuguese Man O'War. The beach was strewn with dead ones, and the way their dark-blue fluted hems waved in the breeze made them look like bedraggled party decorations the morning after.

Soon the water between rollers was up to their waists. This was Gulf-water, dark murky green with reddish sand stirred up in it so that we couldn't see our submerged parts. We could feel the soft smooth bottom and strange things brushing against our calves. Somewhere, I knew, there were rays and sharks, but you couldn't let that spoil your fun. The kids clung to me for a bit, put their arms around my waist or my neck. I taught them oncoming wavery: how to dive under them and come out the back side, how to dive over them, how to stand and let them shove you over backward. My last lesson was how to eyeball a big one coming in and dive on your stomach so that you rode it in until your belly and knees scraped on the bottom. Once they tried that, they lost their fear and moved away from me. Then I had to warn them about going out too far.

Later, we all strolled along the beach when the sun was lower and the wind had died down a little. Janice and I ambled along, holding hands, while Keith and Nicole trotted like sniffing puppies from item to item, failing to discriminate between oil-rig debris like hunks of yellow rope and shells or sand dollars.

I felt at peace. I was thinking about how Janice and I had come to the beach right after we were married and slept in the back of a station wagon I had borrowed from my parents and tried to make love but we were both hot and sticky and salty and the mosquitos attacked us mercilessly. A few years after that we had come during a summer of graduate school and rented a motel suite with another couple; the husband I later suspected to be Janice's lover. Walking along the beach, holding her hand, all that seemed remote, partly because my own affair of only a few months past, already confessed to, had established an equilibrium. Our time together at the ranch had, like the time we spent in Mexico, brought us back together.

Then we cooked hot dogs and beans on the Coleman stove. We also built a small fire from driftwood to roast marshmallows by and for atmosphere. Getting beds laid out in the van and then serving the hot dogs as the kids stood eagerly holding up paper plates, I recalled my own childhood, when my family went camping in the mountains in New Mexico, how good any kind of food tasted to me after a long day of hiking or swimming or breathing fresh air. Here was a link, a continuity, and I seemed very grown-up to myself playing Father at the Beach, just the way my own father had.

As the sun was going down, the gulls came in and wheeled overhead while we ate. The kids tossed bits of hot-dog bun into the air and the gulls flocked and dove just over our heads to snatch the morsels before they fell; they squawked and screamed and wheeled over us like a volatile storm cloud while the kids teased and coaxed them into maneuvers like little conductors.

I could say here that then, in the darkness, in the firelight, I told stories, and maybe I did. I *hope* I did, but I would not be able to say for certain what they were. I do remember there was very little moonlight, and later when the fire died, we sat and waited to hear little scurrying sounds a few yards away where some of the bread bits tossed to the gulls had landed. When we flicked on the flashlight, there were a couple of kangaroo rats sitting up on their little haunches; then they bounded away. We laughed. Each time we waited and then turned on the light, it was like the opening of the Kangaroo Rat Show, tiny top hats and canes, with a couple of skittish sand crabs as a chorus line.

Of course, nobody slept much. It's best not to expect it. Keith and Nicole complained about not being comfortable, fretted, argued with each other about who had the best place. The wind died, the temperature and humidity rose and the mosquitos came whining out of the dunes to attack us in force. But still, they can't keep you up *all* night, and I awoke around dawn to see a pinch of the orange sun glimmering over the tranquil waters of the Gulf. I got up, built a fire, put on the coffee, then walked down to the beach to see what the tide had brought in during the night. After I had walked about a half mile, I looked back down the beach to where the van was parked, nestled among the dunes, only its nose visible. I remember imagining that I was a stranger walking on the beach and that a family was sleeping in the van. I was both places at once. Thinking of "that family" that way made us seem small and vulnerable.

Later that afternoon, when we had grown weary of the sun and salt and sand, we went into Corpus and rented a motel room to clean up and nap in. The air-conditioning alone was worth the price of the room. Hot showers, clean sheets—it was lovely. As we drew the shades to make the room dark to nap in, I thought it was too bad that the kids were there in the room with us. I tried to recall if this was the same motel we had stayed in when we made the trip to the beach with the other couple. Even so, it made no difference—it was nice that all our troubles were over.

After our naps, we put on our best togs—clean shorts and clean pullovers or t-shirts—and went to the best restaurant in town. I remember how we later spent another night on the beach, played the next day in the water and waited until early evening to leave for home so we wouldn't have to be driving in the heat. After it got dark, the storms rolled in from the southwest, along with high winds and rain that buffeted and shook the old broad bus as we crept along blinded by darkness and rain. The radio told us about how tornadoes were being sighted nearby. Out of the darkness would come an unexpected, dazzling flash followed by booms and crashes, and the light would briefly illumine the burly and ugly stratocumulus to the west of us closing in like a mountain range on the march. I hoped that I would see the funnel cloud silhouetted in the background on a flash like that or I could pull off the road and we could run for a ditch. I was scared and couldn't show it; I was responsible for everybody's safety but felt helpless to secure it.

The evening before, we had waited in the crowded foyer of the restaurant with people dressed in skirts and slacks and jackets. The restaurant was no three-star affair, but it overlooked the bay and had tablecloths and you knew it was where the local Episcopalians came after church to eat the shrimp dinner. When we were led through a crowded dining room I felt a little embarrassed for us. But we held our heads up and ordered to the end of our budget, for the point was to Introduce the Kids to Seafood. We explained ourselves to our waitress, and we were overheard at a nearby table occupied by three elderly women. One of them said to me, "My grandchildren will eat seafood but only if it's fried." The women had large straw purses they set beside their chairs; two of them were wearing polyester pantsuits in pastel hues, and the third had on a denim skirt with huge embroidered flowers on it.

They kept watching us, smiling at us, as we took our platters and explained the items to Keith and Nicole. They waited with us for reactions. We were a little like a show for them to watch. Maybe they were remembering how it was before their husbands died, how it was when their kids were still at home. I thought they knew that we were poor;

I thought they thought that we were an awfully nice family. Poor but clean. I remember how much I relished the pleasure of knowing at that moment how much we looked alike, how my handsome twins were so obviously brother and sister, how they looked so much like both of us. We were one of those families who looked like they all belonged to each other, and I was proud.

The message in my first fortune cookie—"A friend soon will bring you money"—seems irrelevant to my desires and needs. I slip the other cookie into the pocket of my sport coat and go to the register counter to pay our bill.

Nicole's sitting in my car with the windows down, working on what is probably her second or third Marlboro. When she sees me coming, she tosses what's left into the gutter. I get into the driver's seat and make a big production by waving my hands, saying, "Cough! Cough! Hack! Jesus, that stinks! How can Zack stand that smell? Did you ever hear—"

"Yeah, I know. 'Kissing somebody who smokes is like licking an ashtray.' "

I laugh. "You've heard it, then."

I hand her the other fortune cookie, and she breaks it open, nibbles on a half, uncoils the fortune. As we're moving out into traffic, I decide that I'm not going to just sit on my resentment about being abandoned back there, and I'm not going to pretend that the American tobacco companies are to blame, either.

"I have a bone to pick with you. I think it's rude of you to get up and leave me sitting there by myself when I really don't get to spend that much time with you, anyway. It would seem to me that you could just hold off smoking or do it in front of me."

"I'm sorry," she says. She sounds sincere. She looks

down at the uncoiled fortune spread between her hands.

"What's it say?" I ask.

"You will get AIDS because you made your dad mad," she says.

"You didn't make me mad," I say. "You hurt my feelings."

"Whew, Dad, come on! No guilt trips!"

"I believe in guilt trips, you know that. I think if you can make somebody feel guilty it must be because they are guilty, you know, the smoke and fire stuff. If people have done something wrong, they should feel guilty. You and Keith both think that when you feel guilt you should try to get rid of it, but I say it's a valuable fuel. Some of our most amazing achievements have come from people convinced that they were utterly worthless and perpetually guilty. Don't underrate it."

She knows I'm joking now and laughs. After a moment, she reaches into the back seat, retrieves her book bag and digs out a notebook she will need in the library. We lapse into a companionable silence, and I turn the radio on to an FM classical station, poke into the middle of a harpsichord tinkling that sounds like Scarlatti. Nicole doesn't complain any more or fight with me about which station we're going to listen to, and now and then she'll even venture a question about the music I've chosen. Sometimes the realization that they really do grow up astonishes me. I hum; I feel light-hearted, buoyant—being with her when she's in a good mood makes me feel good in turn, partly because that's when I really know she's safe and happy, but I don't like for my moods to be so dependent on hers. Keith brings out the drill sergeant in me and makes me feel like a mentor; he can also make me furious. But only Nicole can hurt my feelings yet still make me feel like clowning.

# ELEVEN

## Restoration

"Aw, come on, Dad! Where's your Christmas spirit?"

Keith and I are standing in a raw wind, feet mired in gooey black clay, looking at a display of trees in a vacant lot. Overhead a string of lights sways in the gusts. The tree he wants is about my height—his height, too, now that he's fifteen—but the tag says sixty dollars.

"How about this one?" I point to a stubby but nicely shaped tree about as tall as, well, Dr. Ruth. Among its other virtues is its price. "Only twenty-five bucks. That's my idea of what one should cost."

"We always had a big one," he says.

This is a complicated moment. For an instant, I presume that "always" means when I lived with him and Nicole and Janice; then I realize "always" means "since you left." I almost take the bait but hold back, seeing that he could have said *Mom* always had a big one." Then it dawns on me that what he really means is "I'm used to having a big tree and this is just another of the many things that's different about living with you instead of with her, I guess."

"Well, I like big trees too, but I can't remember their ever costing this much. Do you mind too much having a small one?"

"No, it's okay."

Driving away with the tree poking out of the trunk, I realize that we've once again played a quick hand of catch-up: Despite frequent contact and extended periods of visitation, there were many things about this kid I hadn't realized until he moved in with Marcia and me at the end of his school term last spring. I hadn't known he still took a boyish delight in Christmas, a delight in which getting was far less important than the trappings, the rigamarole, the rituals, the liturgy—"The Grinch," *It's a Wonderful Life*— and, rare and gratifying, the pleasures of giving. Every Christmas since the divorce they've come to my house for a meal and the ceremonial opening of presents, but until this year I hadn't noticed how he hums and dances through the malls while going down his list. In this, he's his mother's son—out of my forty-five Christmases, I've enjoyed about six, tolerated a couple dozen, endured the rest. Marcia, who also took him shopping, said that he gets excited when he finds something he knows someone else would like. He relishes their reaction in advance.

For this reason, I'm a little sorry about the tree, but my budget is tight. I didn't want to drag out my list of liabilities just to make him feel guilty, liabilities that include a mortgage on a house bought primarily so that he could come live with us, and a hefty monthly tuition to his private prep school, for which Janice partly pays. I don't want him to feel that he's a burden; I want him to feel that I willingly assume these responsibilities.

He came to live with us because he wanted to, because Janice wanted him to, because I wanted him to. He spent last year, his freshman year, on the brink of failing most of his subjects, so he and Janice and I saw this move as a chance to get a new start under a new, more strict, regime. However, he hadn't been a behavioral problem, really: He simply lacked motivation and self-discipline; he was lazy, and he procrastinated.

The minute he moved in, I began to treat him as a project. Boy oh boy! I thought. At last I have a child to mold in my own image, I get to *practice* my fathering! I can build me a real good son, get myself a merit badge, show the sucker off, get a trophy, maybe, for fathering. I could work my way out of the cellar.

We have butted heads again and again. One of the unsettling things about having your children grow up under your nose is seeing that they have inherited some of your less savory characteristics, in this case a declarative bluntness that is unnecessarily provocative. We have argued about when to do homework and how, whether he should have a job and what kind and when he should be allowed to work at it, how late he may stay up on week nights, how late on weekend nights, how many nights he may spend at other people's houses, how he spends his money, his rights to privacy, his grades. We argue about if, when and how he should be grounded; we argue about how frequently and how unnecessarily he lies to me; we argue endlessly about his not wearing his glasses at school. Janice bought him contacts, but he lacked the grit to get used to them.

I become obsessed with the imperfections in his character and imagine that it's my duty to perfect them. He is the iron, I am the blacksmith, my standards the anvil. I think of his character as still malleable. I focus on what there is that needs changing. He, on the other hand, feels that his character is set, has already solidified permanently, that he is different: "I'm not like you, Dad, not everybody in the world is like you!" He feels that he has already become who he is and that I shouldn't try to change him. He complains that I nag him too much, that I'm too strict, that I don't know how to motivate people, that I only know how to criticize, that nothing he does is good enough for me, that I don't reward him for progress.

True. Well spoken, lad. What I feel a lot of the time is that I'm not too hot at this fathering busness even when my kid is under my own roof. In my zeal to create the perfect person from the unformed clay that is my child, I forget that he's already something and much of that is highly admirable, attractive, something to take paternal pride in, whether credit is due or not. He's very bright, very articulate, extremely personable—I would feel confident in having him be interviewed alone by any adult for any reason because he presents himself so well, has tremendous poise and presence. He walks up to strangers and strikes up conversations; he asserts himself easily at, say, a crowded concession counter. He takes no drugs and has no apprarent interest in alcohol though, like his sister, he does smoke cigarettes. He's generous with his friends and with us, and he's very popular with his classmates. He's had three jobs and enjoys making his own money; he's very tidy and neat; he can be gentlemanly when it's required—"Yes, ma'm"—but he's also capable of mischief. He's served time in detention at his school for hanging a *Playboy* centerfold out of a second-story window. He's the first person up on weekdays at our house, and by the time I rise, he's dressed and is eating a breakfast he fixed for himself. I forget that he's growing up: He wears my socks and sometimes my shirts; astonishingly, the state we live in thinks he's old enough to learn to drive an automobile. When we walk through shopping malls together, young women glance his way and nudge each other with their elbows. This makes me feel old, ugly—and jealous.

Both my children feel I try to make them be like me. Janice lets them be whoever they are or want to be—she's always believed in laissez-faire child-rearing—but I've always had a "hands-on" philosophy. It's ironic, considering that I wasn't present to put my hands on but she was there to keep hers off.

"Why does everybody have to be like you?" says Nicole after I've reprimanded her for being messy or late or forgetful. "Why does the whole world have to conform to your program?"

"Not everybody does," I say. "Only my children."

Maybe I have a greater need than many fathers to form their characters just to prove to myself that I was there. Sometimes my children seem to have more personality material that could be worked on than do most children. I don't mean that they have more flaws: They have "loud" personalities with many edges and quirks and idiosyncrasies all festooned in a positively baroque fashion, with silly notions and preferences; they are full of passions they feel must be acted upon and cripple-witted opinions they are certain have to be expressed. And their father is a man who feels uncommonly obliged to correct them. This is a recipe for conflict.

I worry about Keith, about how much he brags, about his lies. I hold gala Worry Fests over diverse and varied aspects of his life, the way he will not do anything difficult or undesirable unless he's nagged, the way he refuses to believe that his grades are more important than any other aspect of his present life, the way he seems to treat girls with an off-handedness that sometimes amounts to callous indifference—"Listen, I'm about to do my homework—

can you call me back in about thirty minutes?" Sometimes at two in the morning I slip into my very comfortable Worry Wear and stay up for a while meditating on the many Marlboros he smokes while sitting in the porch swing talking to his friends on his cordless phone. Speaking of talking, I worry that he doesn't talk to *me* enough about things that are bothering him; he sometimes tells them to Marcia, knowing that she will probably relay them to me.

At my Worry Fests, I devote much time to Upcoming Concerns, such as graduating on time from high school, getting into college, driving an automobile safely, becoming self-supporting. I am a one-man Worrying Band, a calliope of off-key sounds he hears as a corny, ole-time music. I clang trash can lids and grunt to make a horrific music designed to get his attention. I chant: *If you don't do this now, then later you won't get to, be able to. . . .* I live in his future partly because he seems so wholly uninterested in it. I huff and pant and talk myself blue—or red—in the face about getting homework done, about eating something green now and then. I don't talk to him about using condoms and worry that I should. *Things are different these days, Dad, they're not the same as they were when you were growing up.*


After we set the tree up beside the fireplace in the living room and decorate it, it doesn't look bad at all. Keith approves.

"Looks great," he says. "Where's the train? You going to put the train up?"

When my brother was a child, he got a Lionel electric train one Christmas, and a few years back it came into my possession, so I started putting it around the Christmas tree in the other house. I put a Santa in the caboose and loaded all the gondolas and flatbed cars with candy and nuts.

"We don't have room here," I say.

"Aw, come on, Dad, where's your Christmas spirit?"

"We'd be stepping all over it for the next two weeks," I argue.

His enthusiasm for the season continues to amaze me as the days go by. He shops with zest for his grandparents, carefully budgeting money from the paychecks he receives from working at a neighborhood theater. It pleases me that he's willing to spend all his savings and his current wages on presents, but I caution him against spending too much.

About a week before Christmas, he has completed his shopping and, aided by Marcia, has wrapped his presents and arranged them artfully under the tree. Sometimes now I can go into the living room and catch him on his knobby knees rearranging packages, rattling some, pressing on them, listening to them.

"Hey, Dad, check this out." He hands me a package about the size of a shoe box. It's to me from him and Nicole. "What do you think it is, huh?"

"I don't know," I say.

"Hey, I bet you wish you did, huh? You're gonna really love his, Dad. This isn't going to be like that English Leather we got you that you never used . . ."

"Yes, I did."

"Hey, it's still up there in your medicine cabinet—it's been four or five years! And how about that shaving kit we got you year before last, with the mug and the razor that matched?"

"Well, I use that too sometimes."

He waves away my lies good-naturedly. "It doesn't matter, because *this* time we got you something you can actually use!"

"What is it?" I grin.

In mock indignation, he takes the package from my hands and puts it back under the tree. "Hey, you'll just have to wait to find out."

The next day, at dinner, he says, "So what do you think we got you, huh?"

"Gee, I don't know."

"Oh, come on, guess!"

I try out a few guesses calculated to be wildly improbable. I don't want to accidentally guess and have to see his disappointment. I have no earthly idea what it might be. So far as I know, I have everything I need.

By Christmas Eve day, he's still coaxing me into the living room to take still another look, and now he can't resist dropping hints. I can see that he's rearranged all the presents again.

"It's something you can use for your work," he offers.

"Good," I say.

"So what do you think it is?"

A bunch of #2 pencils? "I just don't know."

"Well, you're really going to like this."

He's gone through this same routine with Marcia. And when his grandparents arrive in the afternoon, he gives them a preview of their gifts, too, before going off to spend the night at Janice's with Nicole. This heretofore unseen aspect of his personality makes me glow quietly with pride, even though I had no part in encouraging it. It's a nice complement to the impulses toward world peace and universal brotherhood that show up in the lyrics of the songs he writes for the garage band he's in.

As we spend a quiet evening with my parents, my mother shows me the pieces of the family silverware and a set of china she has brought for me to have. Now that she and my father have retired, they have been paring down their possessions and have moved from the house where I grew up into a duplex that they now rent in another city. She used to be a collector, a gatherer of heirlooms and things passed on, but now she seems like someone who wants to travel light for the rest of the trip.

Me, I seem to be taking on the weight. I realize as she talks to me about the silver and the china that even with only three members, my household is the largest in our family west of the Mississippi. Her mother died last year only a short time after my grandmother's sister had died, and the men on that side of the family have long been gone. The children are scattered hither and yon. My father's mother lives alone not too far from her granddaughter and her brood, but my father's brother has died, too, and his widow also lives alone. My brother has been married three times, has no children by any marriage and tends to wander.

So, having recently bought a house, having recently come into full-time, fairly reliable employment and having married my live-in lover and taken in my own son, I am now eligible to assume a role not unlike a patriarch in training, or on probation. We have had Christmases at my house three or four times these past few years. By taking the silver and the china, I am tacitly agreeing to wear the mantle of responsibility and respectability, however tattered it may have become. I am agreeing to become the repository of the family traditions, the man in charge to whom people in the family come. The carver of roast beasts. I always did hanker to be like Tolstoy, and all this business hits me right where it hurts good.

Christmas morning, we adults eat a calm and leisurely breakfast before the kids arrive from Janice's. Then, they're here, only this year I have the comfortable feeling of knowing that Keith is coming home after having been out to

Janice's. We all sit on the living room couch for photographs—my mother and Marcia are the family recorders,
it's women's work—in various arrangements and combi-
nations, and then we begin to open our presents. Nicole
sits beside her grandmother on the couch, dressed quite
prettily in a skirt and sweater, looking healthy and calm,
even chipper, while Keith goes on his knees to the tree
and plays Santa, drawing out the packages and reading off
the names, handing them out. He likes to be in charge of
things, but so do I, and that's why we butt heads so often.
This is one job I'll let him do, though.

Naturally, he teases me with "the" present several times
("Hey, I bet you'd like to open this one now, huh, Dad?
Well, tough, you've got to wait your turn.") before giving
it to me at long last. He's terribly excited about my opening
it and yet he's still reluctant, too, not only because he wants
me to get antsy about it, but the moment the wrapping is
gone, the mystery is over. I tear the paper very slowly,
teasing him back, until I have it unwrapped.

"You like it?"

"Yes," I say. "A lot! Thanks."

I'm not lying. He and Nicole have bought me a battery-
operated revolving address drum that brings up a name or
address at the punch of a button. It is truly something that
I need and will use. That they have finally hit on something
like this is a sign of their maturity.

Later, we all sit at our dinner table to eat the Christmas
ham, sweet potatoes, mashed potatoes, lima beans, cran-
berry, rolls, the etceteras heaped upon our groaning oak
board. I remember how when Janice and I first got married,
we received a lot of silver trays and the like from people
who must have imagined that I'd be a dean in no time.
Janice and I carried that stuff around for a dozen years,
wrapped up in clear plastic that showed how blackened it

had become, before we finally sold it in a garage sale. We were hippies; we liked stoneware. Now, sitting at the head of this table, hosting my children, my parents, looking down at the heirloom silver and china, I feel all patriarchal and "settled," and I'd know what to do with all those silver trays.

I feel a vague urge to give an invocation or say grace; my father has been a churchgoing man all this life, my mother and Marcia and I not at all, but saying grace would be too shocking for everyone but him. Nevertheless, sitting here on this occasion, I wish we all were deeply entrenched in some orthodoxy that would bring a sacred aura to what is otherwise a secular occasion. In lieu of grace, I break out a bottle of wine, pour it into glasses for everyone and offer a toast to us all. Keith and Nicole seem shy and embarrassed about this clinking of glasses—after all, how many times have they ever done it?—and when they taste the wine they grimace, but I'll have to give them this: They sit real straight and polite throughout the meal, and Keith even regales us with a tale about his algebra teacher whom he had nicknamed Mogambo for the sake of this story, no doubt. Even after dessert they sit patiently until they sense they can ask to be excused wihout giving offense. When I see them twitching and sending one another signals across the table, I release them. In our house, these days, it's the children who retire to the veranda for post-prandial cigars.

Later that night, lying in bed, I marvel at the tranquility of the occasion. The Christmas When Nothing At All Remarkable Happened. Sometime in the afternoon, Keith came in from the porch, grinned at us, and said, "Well, Dad, we're going for a walk, we do get bored on these holidays, you know." But he wasn't fretting about it; he was being ironic. "We get bored, too," my father told him. "That's why we eat so much," and in that moment I saw that my father's sense of humor had passed through me and had landed in Keith.

Everyone stayed happy. There were no raised voices, no conflicts; it was as if my children decided that they would unconsciously observe the subtle ceremony of my ascension by bowing to my authority like meek, old-fashioned kids obeying their elders.

I like to think it will be this way more and more as the years go by. Right now I wish we didn't fight so much, my son and I, my daughter and I. I wish we could have more fun merely doing things together, but at this time in our lives, it is both too early and too late. They are fifteen as I write this. And I have to confess that fifteen-year-old people are my least favorite of the species, that much of the time we simply do not like each other.

It has taken me years to realize how natural this is. Our not liking one another is *not* a consequence of my divorcing their mother. I say it is not natural for members of a family to like one another: It's nice if it happens, but really all that's required is for members of a family to take care of each other. It's watching too many episodes of *Little House on the Prairie* that leads you to the false conclusion that "good" families are all composed of people who would have selected each another had they been given the choice. Television producers are able to exploit this wish precisely because it's so rare. It's a condition to admire and envy when you occasionally come across it in life, but it's a mistake to imagine that the condition can be aspired to or achieved. Peace can be achieved; a resolution of conflict can be worked toward; understanding can occur through honest talk and constructive argument; but, to my mind at least, liking can only happen when people are equals and one is not in charge of another, and then it occurs as a mysterious act of mutual chemistry.

I don't expect that my children will even be able to like me until they're grown and don't have to extract my permission for governing their lives. But wondering about whether they'll like me some day implies that I feel confident that they love me. They have been angry, are less so now, and in many ways have forgiven me, though not altogether. I suspect that the future will show me consequences of the divorce that are still unknown to all of us now; as I watch them struggle through their own relationships, I'll always wonder if their problems, whatever they are, can't be traced back to the Fall of 1979 when I became their Uncle Dad. I'm sure they won't be reluctant to identify for me whatever portion of the blame they think is mine. When they have children of their own I'll be aware of how I cheated those children, my grandchildren, out of the opportunity to have the kind of grandparents I enjoyed.

Yet I understand how fruitless and egotistical this search for my territorial boundaries really is. If they are having problems now, if they have problems in the future, the most sensible response should be not "How did I cause them?" but "How can I solve them?" Besides, our life together now seems to have little to do with the divorce, and even less as time passes. Sometimes months go by that we don't mention it, and I cautiously conclude that both my children are so caught up in their own living, exciting present that they seldom think about their early childhood; when they do, they seem to remember good things, funny things, small curiosities and odd little cameos.

But now and then the dagger falls out of the cloak and clatters onto the floor when everybody least expects it. Not long after Keith moved in with us, he was sitting at the dinner table and was explaining that he was supposed to give a speech in class about being afraid. What was he going to talk about? I asked. "About how I'm so scared of thunderstorms," he said. When did he first start being afraid of thunderstorms? "Oh, well, it was when I was real young and we were all living together over on McFarlin," he began, then interrupted himself a moment to think. "No, I think it was later when we were all living in Oak Cliff. No, wait! It was after you and Mom had said you were going to be separated—no, it was after you said you were going to get divorced, that's it! And I was walking back from Corbin's one day when it started to thunder and rain and it scared me, so I started crying and running back home. But when I got there, the house was locked and Mom wasn't home yet. So I had to just stand on the porch and wait for somebody to come."

But my point still holds. For most people, and my children are very much like most people, the present is profoundly more interesting and engrossing than the past. I was a large part of their past; I'm a smaller part of their present, but that is as it should be now. What happened forms a bulge of significance in the lie of our memories, like a knot in a rope, but we're yards past it now. Despite all that I can condemn myself for, I'm also glad that I didn't give up. Although I hurt them and may have damaged their potential for happiness in the future, I'll gladly remain within their range as a target or a sounding post for the next few decades.

I feel that I've earned back some credits, regained some respect. The hair on my shirt has been worn down to the hide.